Copyright

Contents

The man on the platform

A LIFETIME AGO, LONG before the internet, I read a fascinating magazine article about a study that looked at how people stereotype. I haven't been able to track it down online, so I can't cite the source; but here's how I broadly remember it.

An actor walks the platform of a busy London railway station and tells people he can't get home because his wallet has been stolen. He asks for money to buy a train ticket or, at the very least, to make a phone call from a payphone (there were no mobile phones back then).

He does the experiment three times, each time adopting a different persona – first posing as an unsophisticated lower-class man, then as a respectable middle-class man and finally as a distinctly upper-class man. His appearance, demeanour, clothing and accent all reflect the character he is playing.

Can you guess how it turns out?

People are least helpful when he is lower-class, more helpful when he is middle-class and most helpful – even solicitous – when he is upper-class (one person even offers to pay for a taxi).

With nothing else to go on but the way the actor looks, speaks and comes across, it's not surprising that he is put in a mental "box" and judged accordingly. After all, people have probably ten seconds at most to reach a decision. This is stereotyping at its most basic. I have little doubt that the experiment would yield exactly the same results if it were repeated today.

Here's a definition of the word "stereotype" from the well-thumbed, twin-volume 1993 edition of *The New Shorter Oxford English Dictionary* sitting on my bookshelf: "A preconceived, standardized, and oversimplified impression of the characteristics which typify a person, situation, etc., often shared by all members of a society or certain social groups; an attitude based on such a preconception."

This broad definition, expressed in neutral terms without any value judgement, shows that stereotyping applies to all manner of things and not just to people. You can stereotype anything that you have a generalised, oversimplified idea about. You then assign certain characteristics to it.

Another way to view stereotypes is in terms of associations. For example, youth is associated with vigour and vitality, so you're more likely to stereotype a young person as fit and healthy than an old-age pensioner. France is associated with fine cuisine, so you're more likely to stereotype a French person as a good cook than, say, a German. Such associations are rational and statistically valid, and it would be strange indeed to dismiss them as mere stereotypes.

You can stereotype things: Japanese cars have a better build-quality than American cars; European movies are "artier" than Hollywood movies; Italian cuisine is less pretentious than French cuisine.

You can stereotype situations and events: weddings are boring; visits to the dentist are terrifying; sitting in a bar drinking all evening is a sign of an empty life.

You can stereotype animals: dogs are loyal and faithful; cats are aloof and pretentious; snakes are dangerous and best avoided.

You can stereotype an individual: Kevin is from England, so he probably plays cricket; Heather is a woman, so she probably cooks well; Kim is Asian, so he must be good at maths.

You can stereotype groups of people: immigrants to a new country are generally conscientious and hard-working; men are more violent than women; teenagers are unsafe drivers.

You can stereotype countries, restaurants, Taylor Swift songs, John Grisham novels, Scotch whisky, sushi, Korean cars, Australians, BMW drivers, people with tattoos ... the list is endless. All it means is you have an oversimplified, generalised idea of each of these things, and that you assign certain characteristics to them.

Your stereotypes can be highly personal (call-centre agents are useless and never solve your problem) or widely shared (Volvo drivers are courteous and respectful on the road, whereas BMW drivers are pushy and aggressive).

In the case of the man on the platform, three distinct stereotypes are at play: he's poorly dressed, talks funny and looks suspicious – he's probably a hustler trying to con me out of my money; he seems respectable and has an honest look about him – I think I can trust him; he's impeccably dressed, speaks the King's English and has good manners – he's the real deal.

How would *you* have reacted to the man on the platform? Would you have resorted to this kind of stereotyping? Or do you regard yourself as unprejudiced and not given to lazy generalisations? Hold that thought while you do the following short quiz.

1. You're a jury member on the opening day of the trial of a 30-year-old single mother accused of fraud and

embezzlement. She is blonde and attractive, somewhat shy, and has an endearing girl-next-door look about her. What's your gut reaction – guilty or innocent?

2. You're an event manager in charge of catering a wedding. On the big day, the chef wakes up with the flu and is out of action. There are two substitute chefs available. One is from France, the other from England. Who are you more likely to choose – the French chef or the English chef?

3. You're an airline check-in agent. The flight is about to depart, and you have discretionary power to offer a free business-class upgrade. There are two passengers left in line: a well-dressed, preppy-looking man carrying a laptop and a copy of *The Wall Street Journal*; and a sassy, gum-chewing woman wearing a tight T-shirt, figure-hugging jeans and high heels, and carrying a copy of *People* magazine. Who are you more likely to offer the upgrade to – the man or the woman?

4. Your ailing, elderly grandmother needs to be looked after at home with love, empathy and understanding. Two competent, equally qualified candidates apply for the job. One is a man, the other is a woman. Who are you more likely to choose – the man or the woman?

5. You're interviewing for an executive position in your company. You're down to the last two candidates, both women, and both equally experienced and qualified. One is plump and rather plain; the other is attractive and has an enviable figure. Who are you more likely to choose – the attractive one or the plain one?

Gotcha! You stereotype after all. This doesn't make you a bad person – it just makes you human. Everyone stereotypes, including those most vehemently opposed to it.

We are all different from each other physically, mentally, culturally and in so many other ways. Stereotyping is the first superficial insight into these differences, and it is only normal to seize upon them in forming a first impression. How else would you select a potential date on Tinder?

It is simply not possible to keep track of every single detail of every single person out there or know their life circumstances intimately, so some degree of generalisation and categorisation is necessary. This leads to a kneejerk reaction that predisposes us – often in the blink of an eye – to preferring one person over another. Something in them resonates deep within us, speaking to our hopes, our fears, our values, our culture and everything that makes us who we are. It's an implicit bias or pre-judgement, and it guides our decision-making.

We can choose to follow that bias (which causes us to discriminate) or we can override it for a more open-minded decision. The choice is ours. Bias merely points us in a certain direction; it cannot forcibly take us all the way there. On reflection, we might yet choose the English chef over the French chef, or a man to look after grandma rather than a woman. However, it's not easy because bias often runs deep, operating at an unconscious level. It constantly pulls us towards that which is safe and familiar, keeping us from making decisions that may not be in our best interests.

Bias is particularly valuable in life-threatening situations, where we don't have time to weigh things up from all possible angles. It's why, for example, we instantly become wary when we encounter somebody who looks threatening or suspicious, even though that person may be totally harmless. This over-re-

sponsiveness is sometimes called the smoke-detector principle, a reference to the tendency of smoke detectors to go off at
the slightest whiff of smoke, even when no fire is present. It is
a deliberate part of the design and ensures that a real fire will
not be ignored.[1]

Of course, stereotypes are not always accurate. Being oversimplified generalisations, they necessarily come with a margin
of error. Then again, opinion polls also come with a margin
of error. They are based only on a sample of people rather
than the entire population, yet their findings are extremely
useful. Even the jury system is based on reasonable doubt, not
absolute certainty. In the real world, time and information are
limited, and nobody has perfect knowledge of anything. So,
we make decisions that are satisfactory rather than optimal
– in other words, good enough rather than perfect. This is
sometimes known as bounded rationality, a term coined by
American political scientist and Nobel laureate Herbert A. Simon.[2]

In an article in *Psychology Today* entitled "Stereotype Accuracy: A Displeasing Truth", author and clinical psychologist
Noam Shpancer Ph.D. argues that the fact that stereotypes are
often harmful does not detract from their reliability as a useful
source of information. He writes: "That stereotypes are often
accurate should not be surprising to the open and critically
minded reader. From an evolutionary perspective, stereotypes
had to confer a predictive advantage to be elected into the
repertoire, which means that they had to possess a considerable degree of accuracy – not merely a 'kernel of truth'."[3]

A prominent advocate for the general accuracy of stereo-
types is Lee Jussim, a professor of social psychology at Rutgers
University and author of *Social Perception and Social Reality:
Why Accuracy Dominates Bias and Self-fulfilling Prophecy.*

In an article in the online magazine *Aeon*, titled "Truth in Stereotypes", Jussim writes: "Although there is some evidence of inaccurate national and political stereotypes, in general, evidence for stereotype accuracy has been trickling in for 40 years, and has become so overwhelming that even social scientists who might prefer to do so are finding it hard to simply ignore or deny."[4]

Categorising people according to their perceived similarities and characteristics is deeply embedded in the human psyche. It comes to us as naturally as breathing and requires no formal instruction. Studies show that as early as age three, long before they've had a chance to be socialised by their environment, the media or society, children have already internalised various stereotypes around ethnicity, gender and attractiveness.[5] According to research by the Max Planck Institute of Neurobiology, the ability to categorise sensory stimuli is crucial for survival in a complex environment. Memorising categories instead of individual items is faster, more efficient and enables a more flexible behavioural response.[6]

In other words, it's more reliable for the brain to categorise (that is, stereotype) red apples as sweeter than green apples instead of trying to recall the taste of every apple ever eaten, which would take forever. This logic applies even more to people, who are infinitely more complex and varied than apples.

This is why the man on the platform was systematically stereotyped by everyone he encountered. It could not have been otherwise.

Is this fair? Is it right not to help a man in need simply because of the way he comes across? Is it okay to prefer one person over another for reasons that may have little to do with their true worth?

The blunt answer is that stereotyping is an automatic brain function that happens whether we like it or not, so our feelings on the subject are irrelevant. A more considered view is that stereotyping is a complex phenomenon that doesn't lend itself to neat and tidy judgements of right and wrong. As the quiz showed, it takes place across many different dimensions simultaneously, always in a specific context and not necessarily with malicious intent. One person's blatant discrimination is another person's rational judgement.

Welcome to the fascinating world of stereotypes!

1

Attractiveness

IF THE MAN ON the platform in the previous chapter had been incredibly handsome, you can be sure that people would have been shoving money into his hands, irrespective of the character he was playing.

And that's because there's nothing like a beautiful face – male or female – to weaken our defences and make us favourably disposed towards the person behind it. Beauty is not necessarily in the eye of the beholder; its roots run much deeper.[1] Studies have shown that newborn infants, some not even two months old, prefer gazing at attractive faces rather than unattractive ones.[2]

Researchers across all cultures reckon the preference for beautiful faces is probably innate. The many criteria include facial symmetry, facial volume, and the size and relative position of the eyes. Plastic surgeons use a centuries-old concept known as the golden ratio to determine what constitutes a harmoniously proportioned face.[3] We can gauge beauty even at a subliminal level after just a split-second look at someone's face.[4]

Beauty is the thin end of the wedge of physical attractiveness, which takes in the entire body and is thought to be an indicator of health and fertility.[5] Men tend to be attracted to younger-looking women with full breasts and a low waist-to-hip ratio (also known as an hourglass figure).[6] Women are attracted to taller men with good upper-body strength, generally signalled by broad shoulders, a slim waist and a V-shaped torso.[7]

When you've got the whole package – a great-looking face and an attractive body – then you've hit the jackpot, physically speaking. You will be favourably perceived and enjoy a tremendous stereotype advantage in life.[8]

Attractive people have always known this; the rest of us accept it with varying degrees of grace, equanimity or envy. The constant positive attention helps them to build confidence and self-esteem early in life and develop valuable social skills. This gives them an edge over their average-looking or less attractive rivals.

I can still recall an incident many years ago in which an attractive, elegantly attired blonde was standing by her car, somewhat embarrassed. It had stalled at the roadside in upmarket Sandton, Johannesburg's main financial district. It seemed as if every male driver going by slowed down to ask her if she needed help. They included corporate types in expensive cars who ordinarily would not be bothered to play the good Samaritan. Even I slowed down, brandishing my cell phone through the window. But she just flashed everyone a bashful smile to indicate she was okay and that help was on the way. Of course, this just made her more endearing. It was a classic damsel-in-distress scenario, and there was no shortage of knights in shining armour – and shining BMWs. Would the response have been as enthusiastic if it had been an unkempt, chubby, average-looking woman in sweatpants?

The existence of a so-called beauty premium,[9] or pretty privilege,[10] is well documented. In the workplace, attractive people are more likely to get hired, to get better job evaluations and to be paid more.[11] By virtue of their looks, they attract more attention and are likely to be offered more opportunities, all of which reinforces their self-confidence. It's a self-perpetuating loop of positivity. Attractive people even find it easier to get venture-capital funding for their start-ups.[12]

In mock jury trials, depending on the charges faced, attractive defendants are less likely to be found guilty and more likely to be given a lighter sentence.[13] A study found that good-looking waiters and waitresses got bigger tips. Interestingly, this generosity was driven mainly by female customers tipping attractive waitresses more.[14] Waitresses in search of higher tips are advised to wear ornamentation in their hair (like a barrette or a flower) because it makes them look more attractive.[15]

Studies in the US[16] and Sweden[17] have found that attractive students are more likely to get better grades. They are generally viewed as smarter than their less attractive peers and are held to a higher standard.[18] Looking back at the many business-writing workshops I used to run during my corporate career, I realise (OMG!) that I often gave more attention to attractive women in the class. It showed in subtle ways like more smiling, more eye-contact and a friendlier demeanour.

In politics, research in several countries has found that good-looking candidates running for election generally win more votes, whether they are male or female.[19] Attractiveness is thought to be particularly important for uninformed or disinterested voters; it is easy to observe and gives them something to go on. Politicians involved in scandals are treated less harshly by voters and public opinion if they are attractive.[20]

Attractive people are often associated with other desirable qualities. If you're attractive, you might be assumed to be trustworthy as well as intelligent, hardworking and competent. You might even be assumed to have a successful career and a happy marriage, even though neither may be true. This cognitive bias is known as the halo effect and can create a distorted perception of attractive people.[21]

It is a bias that cuts both ways. If we attribute desirable traits to attractive people, then we attribute undesirable traits to unattractive people. If what's beautiful is good, then what's ugly must be bad. This is the reverse halo effect, or horn effect.[22] For example: this woman is unattractive, so she's probably also unfriendly and unreliable. I don't think I'm going to hire her.

This is also known as lookism.[23] It just doesn't feel right that good-looking people get all the breaks. Something should be done about it. But what?

We can't pass laws stopping them from enjoying the benefits of their good looks. And we can't compel companies to put unattractive people in high-profile positions. In a free market where consumers have a choice, such companies might feel the effect on their bottom line. Would you still watch your favourite TV talk-show if they replaced the attractive host with someone clearly lacking in the looks department? (This is sometimes disparagingly referred to as having a face for radio.) Would you still vote for the unattractive political candidate? Or buy the brand of cosmetic promoted by an unsexy, plain-looking woman?

Much as we might hate to admit it, the world would be uniform and drab without attractive people. They give us something to admire and feel good about. I remember cheering when the masks finally came off after the Covid-19 pandemic, because it was so good to see beautiful faces again.

This is why we watch the movies with the heartthrob actors and actresses, appreciate the airlines with the attractive cabin crew and buy the products endorsed by attractive celebrities. It's why we put on our best clothes in the morning, style our hair and apply make-up – all so that we can present to the world the most attractive version of ourselves.

Psychologist and Harvard University researcher Nancy Etcoff, author of *Survival of the Prettiest: The Science of Beauty*, argues that our preference for attractiveness is rooted in evolutionary instinct, and that it would be futile to try to deny its influence.[24] Her book contests the notion – popular among certain feminists – that beauty is largely a cultural construct[25] fuelled by factors like advertising, the media and the expectations of men.

That said, attractiveness isn't destiny. Your good looks don't guarantee success; they might even lull you into a false sense of security and make you slack off. The world is full of unsuccessful attractive people. Looks give you an edge, but you still have to do the work.

2

Height

Y OUR HEIGHT IS OBVIOUS and visible, and immediately triggers assumptions about you. It's an easy stereotype for
people to latch on to.

So, here's an interesting question: would you rather be tall
and plain-looking or short and attractive? If you're a man, you
would probably choose the former; if you're a woman, the
latter. Here's why.

To be tall – 1.8 m (6 ft) or more – confers an immediate advantage that allows you to see more, reach further and basically
look down on others. For a man, this is an asset. It allows him
to live up to the masculine ideal of strength and power. It also
makes him more desirable to women, who are naturally drawn
to men who are taller than them.[1]

Indeed, when women describe their ideal partner, *tall* is
almost always the first attribute mentioned. Not for nothing has
the term *tall, dark and handsome* become a cliché in women's
romantic fiction, at least in western society at any rate. "Wow,
he's so short and good-looking!" is not something you're likely
to hear a woman say.

A large body of research in psychology, economics and biology has shown that tall men consistently do better in life than
short men.[2] They are healthier, have more successful careers
and perform better in many sports. They occupy more leader-

ship positions, particularly in business and politics. Short CEOs and prime ministers are rare. In his landmark book *Blink: The Power of Thinking Without Thinking*, Malcolm Gladwell polled half of the Fortune 500 companies and found that nearly 60% of their CEOs were taller than 1.8 m (6 ft), compared with barely 15% of the broader US male population.[3] Studies show that in US presidential elections, the taller candidate is more likely to be chosen by voters.[4] For example, Barack Obama was markedly taller than his rival, John McCain, when he was first elected in 2008. Over the sixty-plus years since 1960, eight of the eleven American presidents were 1.8 m (6 ft) or more in height, with Donald Trump being the tallest at 1.9 m (6 ft 3 in).[5]

Of course, being vertically challenged as a man is no obstacle to success in life, but you do have a higher mountain to climb. Examples that spring to mind are Hollywood actors Danny DeVito, Kevin Hart and Tom Cruise – and, of course, former British prime minister Rishi Sunak, who touches the tape at a modest 1.7 m (5 ft 7 in).

Certain male celebrities who lack a few centimetres in the height department have been known to wear shoes with a stacked heel to give them that extra bit of lift.[6] They include singer-songwriter Bono and former French president Nicolas Sarkozy, whose wife is taller than him. There's even a website with the self-explanatory title *CelebHeights.com*.[7]

Some men may go beyond stacked heels to compensate for their lack of height and engage in aggressive, domineering social behaviour. This is known as the Napoleon complex, after the famous – and short – French emperor and military commander, Napoleon Bonaparte.[8] A study on the syndrome found some support for it and noted that shorter men tended to keep more resources to themselves in a game where they had all the power, also known as the dictator game.[9] It could be just coincidence, but three of the most brutal dictators of the 20th century were of below-average height – Vladimir Lenin, Benito Mussolini and Joseph Stalin. The authoritarian Russian leader Vladimir Putin is also on the short side. Most bodybuilders are short,[10] an obvious inference being that a muscular build helps a man to project the dominance that a short stature cannot. Might this be the male equivalent of breast augmentation? The average height of the winner of Mr Olympia, the world's ultimate bodybuilding competition, held annually since 1965, has been just 1.7 m (5 ft 7 in).[11]

One theory behind the relative success of taller men in life is that they benefit not just from the obvious physical advantage of greater reach and height but also from the increased confidence and self-esteem that this brings.[12] Another is that they are inherently smarter,[13] and that taller children do significantly better in cognitive tests from as early as age three.[14] Either way, tall men seem to get all the breaks.

This is particularly true in dating.[15]

From a woman's perspective, a tall man is seen as protective and strong. He makes her feel safe and secure, and this is what women say they value most in a relationship.[16] They ideally like a man to be 20 cm (8 in) taller than they are.[17] A study found that only 4% of women would accept a relationship with a shorter man.[18] How can he make her feel safe and secure if she towers over him?

If above-average height is an asset for a man, it can be a liability for a woman.

It's well known that tall women struggle on the dating front because their height puts men off.[19] A particularly poignant online video titled "Would You Date a Tall Girl?" shows men simply walking away from their potential date when they see just how tall she is.[20] Many tall women settle for dating shorter men, even though it's not ideal.[21] When seeing a tall woman alongside a markedly shorter man, it's hard not to jump to the conclusion that she's with her brother – or worse, her son.

If men glory in strength and power, women glory in beauty and attractiveness – and generous height is not a key requirement for that. Sure, women may wear high-heeled shoes, but that's less about wanting to be tall than wanting to look good.

Research has shown that high heels can make a woman appear more feminine and sexually attractive, while also projecting status.[22] High heels artificially enhance a woman's body shape. They give a distinct lift to her bottom, push out her chest and make her legs look long and slender.[23] Women on public display – whether in the boardroom, on the red carpet or giving a TED talk – are invariably seen in heels, despite the obvious discomfort and difficulty walking around in them.

Finding a suitable partner isn't the only challenge tall women face. They struggle to find a bathtub in which they can stretch out or a shower high enough to allow them to wash their hair without having to stoop. They battle the ergonomics of chairs, beds and airline seats designed for average-sized people and have awkward hugs with their shorter female friends. Tall women also have to deal with pesky comments such as "Wow, you're really tall!" and "You must be good at sports – do you play basketball?"[24]

Heights vary between countries, according to international rankings.[25] For example, average heights for both men and women in Asian countries like Vietnam or the Philippines are much less than in Europe and North America, and typically hover around 1.6 m (5 ft 3 in) or less. The country with the tallest people in the world is The Netherlands, where the average height is 1.8 m (5 ft 11 in).

Nevertheless, the characteristics attributed to tall versus short people remain the same, and this is particularly true for men. Culture doesn't negate the height stereotype because height is such an obvious physical attribute.

3

Weight

CORPULENT, STOCKY, PORTLY, CHUBBY, plump, Rubenesque, plus-size, full-figured, curvy – there's no shortage of euphemisms to describe the state of being fat or overweight.[1] But it still carries a negative stereotype, with a distinct stigma attached to it.

This is especially true for women, who naturally carry a higher percentage of body fat than men. They are also more susceptible to weight-gain and have a much greater risk of becoming obese.[2]

Being fat makes it difficult for a woman to live up to the feminine beauty ideal,[3] one aspect of which is an attractive figure. This matters much less for men, whose masculinity[4] inclines them more towards strength and courage – witness the incredible bulk of Japan's famous sumo wrestlers or the size of your average nightclub bouncer. Society's disapproving gaze on fat women is particularly unforgiving. They are seen as not just overweight but also unattractive and unappealing. This is especially true in western society, where prevailing beauty standards emphasise thinness.[5]

Overweight women are judged more harshly than overweight men, and at lower levels of excess weight. Men start to experience weight stigmatisation at a body-mass index (BMI) of 35, whereas it starts at just 27 for women.[6] When it comes to body image in general, research shows that women judge themselves more harshly than men.[7] This is true even when the women are not overweight and the men are.

When I go swimming at my health club, it never ceases to amaze me how many women – even those with a perfectly acceptable body shape – cover themselves up with a towel as soon as they emerge from the water. Men, on the other hand, just can't be bothered. Even if they're wearing skimpy Speedo swimwear, they brazenly flaunt their out-of-shape bodies without the slightest hint of self-consciousness. In my entire life, I've never seen a man cover himself up with a towel on emerging from the water. Could it be that women are their own harshest critics? Or is it just in their nature to be modest in public, especially in the presence of roving male eyes?

Contributing to the negative stereotype around excess weight is the matter of responsibility. If someone is short or average-looking, nobody blames them because they were born that way. But no one is born fat – at least not unless they have some kind of genetic predisposition towards obesity. Fat is something you become. Ergo: it must be your fault.

Again, this is particularly true for women. Consciously or unconsciously, the sight of an overweight woman makes us think she eats too much and probably never exercises. The possibility that her condition might be due to social, financial or medical reasons doesn't cross our minds.[8]

However, even allowing for mitigating factors, overweight people – both men and women – are not necessarily off the hook. It might not be their fault, says the court of public opinion, but it is their responsibility. They should do something about it.

In a University of Illinois study, a representative sample of 800 people were asked: Who is primarily to blame for the rise in obesity? A full 94% of them said it was the individuals themselves.[9] Research by University College London found that weight stigmatisation was present even among healthcare professionals, many of whom saw obese people themselves as largely responsible for their plight, rather than any social or environmental factors.[10] According to an internet study done in 10 different countries, there is an increasingly negative attitude towards overweight and obese people.[11] An article in *Psychology Today* commenting on the study refers to a "global aversion to fat people", who are seen as "aesthetically distasteful".[12]

This generally negative attitude is prevalent even among children. In a documentary on weight stigmatisation on Swiss television (RTS) titled *"Grossophobie: Dans la tête d'un gros"*, six sweet, shy-looking girls and boys between four and six years of age are shown three pictures of identical-looking children – one of normal weight, one fat and one in a wheelchair. When asked questions such as who they'd like to have as a best friend, who they'd like to invite to their birthday party or who could help them with their maths, they systematically exclude the fat child – it just seems self-evident to them.[13]

Discrimination against fat people – particularly women – is well documented. They find it harder to get a job, earn less and get passed over for key positions, particularly in client-facing roles. A slender figure is prized for women at executive level, and overweight female CEOs are rare.[14]

The same is true in politics, where research has shown that the slender candidate generally gets a greater share of the vote.[15] Overweight women are even less likely to hold political office than their heavier male or thinner female rivals.[16]

The visibly corpulent Angela Merkel, the long-running chancellor of Germany from 2005 to 2021, was a notable exception. However, she wasn't always that size and was already a known quantity in German politics. Merkel stood in sharp contrast to most French female politicians.[17] With their trim figures, fashionable attire and seemingly effortless chic, they shore up the already favourable stereotype of the slender French woman – witness the global success of the book *French Women Don't Get Fat: The Secret of Eating for Pleasure* by Mireille Guiliano. Examples that spring to mind are Christine Lagarde, president of the European Central Bank, and Élisabeth Borne, prime minster of France from 2022 to 2024.

Overweight women face unfriendly service when shopping for clothes. A study by UCLA's Anderson School of Management in California has found that they experience interpersonal hostility on the part of female sales staff in the form of less smiling, subtle rudeness and a general unwillingness to be helpful.[18]

They find it particularly tough on the relationship front. Just as women prefer not to date short men, men prefer not to date fat women. Among other reasons, they say it would hurt their social status. A sexy, physically attractive woman in a man's life draws admiration from his peers; the opposite is true for a fat woman.[19]

The generally negative perception of excess weight worldwide suggests that the stereotype may well be hardwired in us.

A compelling reason is that being overweight is not good for one's health. It causes medical conditions ranging from high-blood pressure and diabetes to coronary heart disease. Nearly three million people die every year from being overweight or obese, according to the World Health Organisation – and the problem is getting worse.[20]

Could it be that the negative stereotype around excess weight is nature's way of discouraging it so that it doesn't threaten the healthy propagation of the human species? And is the stereotype so much harsher on women because it is they who bear the children? Food for thought.

4

Gender

A KEY DRIVER BEHIND stereotyping is difference, and nowhere is this more striking than in the differences between men and women. Consider the following scenario.

It's late at night and you're walking down a deserted street. You suddenly hear footsteps behind you. You quicken your pace, but so does the person behind you. You take a deep breath, turn around and notice it's a woman desperately trying to catch up with you.

Phew! You breathe a sigh of relief. Threat averted. She asks if she can walk with you because she doesn't feel safe in this neighbourhood.

If it were a man trying to reach you like that, you'd probably go on heightened alert and perhaps even break into a run. After all, he could be a mugger. But that's not something women typically do. So, in a split-second, your senses give you the all-clear.

As a species, we are probably hardwired to recognise that women represent less of a physical threat than men. It's simple biology.

Women are shorter and more delicately built, with softer skin and smaller hands. They are more sensitive to pain[1] and cold[2]. With far less muscle-mass than men, they have only about half of the upper-body strength and two-thirds of the lower-body strength.[3] Men outperform women in championship sport. They run faster in athletics, lift more in weightlifting, and hit the ball harder in tennis and further in golf.

Women behave differently, too.[4] They are less physically aggressive than men. They don't engage in fistfights or brawls, and express anger verbally rather than physically.[5] Enemies aren't beaten up; they are socially excluded or gossiped about. More cautious and fearful[6] than men, women are less likely to take extreme risks or engage in activities that could lead to injury. Men are more prone to alcoholism[7] and anti-social behaviour[8], commit almost all violent crime[9] and account for around 95% of the prison population[10]. Statistically, women are safer drivers than men.[11] They speed less, have fewer accidents and are more likely to obey traffic laws. Men are three times more likely to be killed in road crashes than women, according to the World Health Organisation.[12]

Women are more empathetic and caring. They feel more – and cry more. They are more prone to anxiety and nearly twice as likely as men to be diagnosed with depression.[13] Women are far more attentive to how others are feeling and more inclined to comfort those in distress. Because women bring children into the world, they are hardwired to love, care and nurture in a way men simply cannot.

In the workplace, a woman's management style is generally collaborative and empathetic; a man's is more direct and task-oriented – "just do it".[14] Women build relationships and seek consensus; men take charge and act. A common stereotype in the workplace is that men handle the tough assignments and the brutal negotiations, while women do the soft stuff and keep everyone happy (women are hugely overrepresented in human resources[15] and public relations[16]). Leadership is associated with masculine traits such as confidence and assertiveness, and women who display them get better-paying jobs than their more feminine counterparts.[17] The former no-nonsense British prime minister Margaret Thatcher was called the Iron Lady precisely because she embodied such masculine traits. Not for nothing was she dubbed "the best man in the Cabinet".[18]

Female students at university are more likely to choose soft-skill careers such as teaching, healthcare and languages and account for most of the graduates in these fields.[19] Male students, on the other hand, account for the overwhelming majority of graduates in the STEM fields (science, technology, engineering and mathematics)[20], which also happen to pay more. The Institute for Fiscal Studies in the UK has found that women are generally overrepresented in degree subjects with low financial returns.[21]

A recent joint British-American study analysed the career aspirations of half a million teenagers across 80 countries. In all of the regions surveyed, girls were biased towards people-oriented careers, while boys were biased towards things-oriented careers or those in the STEM fields.[22] Unexpectedly, this trend was even *more* pronounced in the Nordic countries, ranked as the most egalitarian in the world, and has been dubbed the gender-equality paradox.[23]

Many jobs play to the stereotypical differences between men and women. Examples are the caring fields, such as nursing and nannying; the brute-strength fields, such as construction and furniture removal; and the down-and-dirty fields such as plumbing and auto repair. When was the last time a woman plumber came to your house to replace an underground pipe or fix a leaking toilet? The work is physically demanding, strenuous and dirty. In the US, women account for less than 4% of all plumbers.[24] Similarly, if you ever end up in hospital, you're unlikely to be looked after by a male nurse; men make up barely 12% of the profession.[25]

Men glory in strength and power; women glory in beauty. Almost all bodybuilders in the world are men, and they toil for hours at a time in the gym building their muscles.[26] Almost all cosmetic surgery in the world is done on women, common procedures being breast augmentation, facelifts and liposuction.[27] If you want to compliment a woman, tell her how beautiful she looks or how flattering her outfit is; if you want to compliment a man, tell him how big and strong he looks, and perhaps suggest that he's been working out.

One could go on, but a pattern is emerging.

Male/female differences have been extensively studied for more than a hundred years across countries, cultures and continents, and the core findings are always the same.[28] More recent research in neuroscience using brain-scanning technology shows that the brains of men and women are wired differently, and that this may contribute to differences in both behaviour and cognition.[29] The cumulative weight of all this evidence helps to explain why men and women so often have different motivations and interests, and make different life choices. As the American stand-up comedian Elayne Boosler once noted: "When women are depressed, they eat or go shopping. Men invade another country. It's a whole different way of thinking."[30]

These differences have been popularised in bestselling books such as *Men Are From Mars, Women Are From Venus* by John Gray, and *Why Men Don't Listen and Women Can't Read Maps* by Allan and Barbara Pease.

Debate continues on whether these differences are purely physical and biological or whether social, cultural and economic factors also come into play.[31]   Men lean towards the former explanation and women towards the latter. That's according to a survey by the Pew Research Center, which notes that the debate over the reasons for gender differences is "far from settled".[32]

Nevertheless, the differences are there, and they are what drive the stereotypes – and, by extension, the way in which the two sexes perceive and treat each other. After all, if men and women were exactly the same, gender stereotyping could not exist.

5
Age

A LONGSIDE GENDER, AGE IS the most obvious physical mark-
er that tells us what kind of person we're dealing with.
Their age immediately puts them in a box that shapes our
perceptions and expectations. This is age-stereotyping, and we
practise it all the time.[1]

You would not ask a child for directions, a teenager for
relationship advice or an eighty-year-old to help you navigate
your new iPhone. And the reason you wouldn't is because you
are intuitively guided by the stereotype of each age-group.
Imagine all the time you'd waste and the stupid decisions you'd
make without this reliable inner compass.

Let's take a walk through the key stages of ageing and the
stereotypes they project.

When you see a toddler who's perhaps five years old, it's
clear they don't pose any physical threat. You aren't instinc-
tively cautious or mistrustful. You may even playfully touch
them or ruffle their hair. Their knowledge of the world is limited and you might talk down to them. You keep your language
simple and interact with them at their level.

Once boys and girls hit their teens, they start maturing
both physically and sexually. Boys in particular get bigger and
stronger. These rapidly evolving beings are in the full flush
of hormonal transformation, and you are more on your guard

now, if only at a subconscious level. It's why youth violence in all its various forms – crime, assault, sexual violence – is an integral part of national crime statistics, and almost exclusively male.[2] Although teens are not yet fully functioning adults, you start to interact with them on a higher level intellectually. You expect more of them as they start to take responsibility for their lives.

Next comes emerging adulthood, and it's here that stereotypes begin to harden. If older people battle ageism[3], young people between the ages of 18 and 25 battle "youngism"[4] – the perception that they're clueless about real life and what it means to be a responsible member of society. Sure, they might be intelligent and tech-savvy, but they're also sometimes seen as lazy, entitled and disrespectful.[5] Jonathan Haidt, social psychologist and co-author of *The Coddling of the American Mind*, is a well-known proponent of the view that children have been mollycoddled and indulged by their parents, and that they lack the grit and resilience of earlier generations.[6]

This is not a recent observation. Back in 2013 already, *Time* magazine ran a cover story on millennials titled "The Me Me Me Generation" that described them as lazy, entitled narcissists who still live with their parents.[7] A few years later, in 2016, bestselling business author and motivational speaker Simon Sinek said in a controversial interview – viewed some 13 million times online – that millennials are tough to manage in the workplace, and that employers find them entitled, narcissistic, self-interested, unfocused and lazy.[8]

Criticism of young people isn't new. Back in the 16th century, French scholar Henri Estienne noted: *"Si jeunesse savait, si vieillesse pouvait."*[9] Broadly translated: "If youth only knew; if old age only could."

The human brain matures fully only around age 30, so it's perhaps unfair to expect young people to be wise and responsible.

In any event, this lack of life experience has practical consequences. If you're under 25, you'll pay more for a rental car because you're a greater risk on the roads.[10] If you own a car, insurance companies will charge you a higher premium for the same reason.[11] You'll find it hard to get that first job because you lack work experience; and when you do, you'll be paid less than equally qualified older people for the same work.[12]

Fortunately, this situation is not permanent. As you shake off your twenties and become a fully functioning adult, your stereotype changes for the better.

By all accounts, you hit the sweet-spot in your thirties.[13] The combined effect of more career experience, money and maturity makes this an exciting period in life. It translates into an inner confidence, dynamism and energy that confers on you a very positive stereotype.

As you enter your forties, you notice the first stirrings of ageist attitudes towards you.[14] You're now officially over the hill, and it shows. Your hair starts to thin, and your middle starts to bulge. On the career front, walking into a new, high-paying job is no longer the breeze it once was.

In your late fifties and early sixties, you notice society's reduced expectations of you. People treat you deferentially, calling you sir or ma'am. They hold doors open and let you go first. This is sometimes called compassionate ageism.[15] In the movies, you become almost invisible in today's youth- and beauty-obsessed culture.[16] As for a romantic comedy featuring your age-group, or a sexually explicit drama, you can forget about it! In the workplace, your experience makes you an asset but it also makes you expensive, and your employer may be tempted to replace you with somebody younger. It's why age-discrimination lawsuits have increased in recent years, putting various Fortune 500 companies in the spotlight and ushering in multimillion-dollar settlements.[17]

Biological differences between men and women also influence age-stereotyping, because the two sexes don't age in the same way. Men seem to age favourably into rugged looks, crinkly eyes and greying temples, projecting a comforting aura of serenity and gravitas. Women, on the other hand, seem to age more harshly, and lose their beauty and sexual attractiveness. The rose that once bloomed firm and proud is suddenly withered and drooping. Women call this the double standard of ageing.[18] It's why you're far more likely to see an elderly man reading the news on television than an elderly woman. In the movies, older men are cast in leading roles far more often than older women.[19] One study has found that the average earnings per film of female movie stars decrease rapidly after age 34, while those of their male counterparts keep rising until a maximum age of 51 and remain stable thereafter.[20]

As the years go by and retirement looms, your stereotype starts to feel like pity. The cashier at the supermarket check-out may helpfully remind you that Wednesdays is pensioner day, when you can get a 10% discount. Soon, your reflexes slow down, your mental strength declines and you start forgetting things. As the comedian George Burns famously put it: "First you forget names, then you forget faces. Next you forget to pull your zipper up and finally, you forget to pull it down."[21]

It's clear from this broad overview that people at different ages don't just look different – they *are* different. They are perceived differently, and this shapes their stereotype.

6
Face

C AN YOU TELL A person's character and personality just by looking at their face? You can, apparently, and science has uncovered many links between the two.[1] The former is thought to drive the latter – in other words, it's your character that supposedly influences the kind of face you have.[2]

This suggests that if you're by nature a kind, friendly person, your face will mirror those qualities. It's likely to be an open, inviting, smiling face with happy eyes. It says: it's okay to engage with me; you will be safe; I am no threat. This is a positive stereotype that draws people in.[3]

It can be a powerful advantage if you're running for political office. Nelson Mandela, South Africa's first black president, was blessed with this kind of sunny disposition, as was former American president Ronald Reagan. Both men exuded charm and good humour and were extraordinarily effective in connecting with people. I can still recall how they lifted the mood of their respective nations at key moments during their time in office.

At the other extreme, if you're chronically ill-tempered and complain all the time, you will probably have a sullen, scowling face characterised by a furrowed forehead, pinched eyebrows and a tight-lipped or downturned mouth. The message here is very different: approach with caution or I might bite your head

off! This is a negative stereotype that pushes people away –
or at least puts them on their guard. As legendary comedian
Groucho Marx put it: "I never forget a face, but in your case,
I'll be glad to make an exception."[4]

Of course, even kind, friendly people can become ill-tempered; and ill-tempered people can become kind and friendly.
But this is a temporary departure from the norm, and the faces
eventually revert to their default appearance. Over time, the
various facial muscles associated with one's mood and tem-
perament give the face its dominant look and feel.

The ability to read a face can help you choose who to strike
up a conversation with at a party. In a clothing store, it can help
you zero in on the sales assistant most likely to help you find
that new suit. In a sales presentation to potential customers,
it might help you identify who will be most receptive to your
pitch.

Of course, you might be totally wrong in your assessment.
They do say you should never judge a book by its cover. Nevertheless, it's a number's game, and most books are a reasonably accurate reflection of their covers. If only for reasons
of survival, it seems inconceivable that human beings would
come into the world without an innate ability to read, however
imperfectly, the faces of the people they interact with.

As far back as 1984, a study from the University of Missouri
had already shown that subjects were in significant agreement
in their willingness to categorise people as "good guys" or
"bad guys" simply by looking at photographs of their faces and
making certain inferences about their features.[5]

More recent research on the psychology of selecting job
applicants has found that three personality traits – power,
warmth and honesty – can be reliably inferred from facial
features.[6] This comes as no surprise to anyone who watches

movies regularly. The powerful politician, the warm-hearted wife or the honest employee are best played by actors and actresses with specific facial features. For example, tough-looking Robert De Niro comes across well as a ruthless Mafia boss; funny Jim Carrey less so. And I can't recall the likeable Meg Ryan ever being successfully cast in the role of a mean, bitchy woman; she's just too sweet and wholesome.

Determining a person's personality and character from their facial features is known as physiognomy.[7] It is enjoying a resurgence on the experimental front on the back of the boom in artificial intelligence and facial-recognition technology.[8] Indeed, machine-learning algorithms now outperform even skilled people in reading faces. They do this by analysing the geometry and morphology of the face in incredibly minute detail and then cross-referencing the findings with the information stored in memory.

Facial recognition is also used in healthcare to diagnose certain diseases and genetic abnormalities, because these leave subtle, tell-tale symptoms on the face.[9] Even we mere mortals can tell if a friend is tired, hung over or sleep-deprived simply by looking at their face because the signs are so obvious.

In one study, a machine-learning algorithm analysed photographs of 25 000 participants and reliably predicted what is known in psychology as the Big Five personality traits – extraversion, agreeableness, neuroticism, openness (to experience) and conscientiousness.[10] Interestingly, it was conscientiousness – the willingness to do one's work or duty well – that was the easiest to predict, for both men and women. Might this one day find its way into hiring practices?

Such algorithms can even reliably predict a person's political orientation. Research from Denmark conducted on thousands of photographs of local politicians found that men and women who appeared happier were more likely to be right-wing; those with a neutral expression were more likely to be left-wing; and women who showed contempt were more likely to be left-leaning.[11] However, similar studies conducted on political figures in the US found that liberals (left-wing) were more likely to have an open, expressive face compared with conservatives (right-wing), who tended to have a more buttoned-down, serious look.[12] This suggests that national culture and norms come into play.

In a large-scale American study, a facial-recognition system analysed online images (from Facebook and popular dating websites) of just over a million people from the US, Canada and the UK. It was able to predict their political orientation (liberal versus conservative) with a level of accuracy of up to 72%, which was much higher than human accuracy or plain chance. A single facial image was reckoned to be much more reliable than having a person fill in a long questionnaire.[13] Might this one day find an application in fields such as election polling and market research?

Another characteristic that can be reliably inferred with just a split-second look at a person's face is competence, or at least the perception of it. That's according to a study by a Princeton University psychologist featured in the journal *Proceedings of the National Academy of Sciences*. Subjects were shown a series of photographs, each containing a pair of faces they didn't recognise, and asked to choose which face came across as more competent. Little did they know that the photographs were of political candidates in the running for state governor or for a seat in the US Senate. The candidates rated as more competent ended up winning around 70% of their respective election races.[14]

So, it turns out that the face really is the mirror of the soul. Even at first glance, it is a mine of information and shapes the way we stereotype each other.

7
Attire

Y OU CAN'T CHANGE YOUR looks; you can't change your height; and you can't change your body shape – but you can change your clothes.

It allows you to shape the image – and hence the stereo-type – you project to the world. No matter what hand you've been dealt in terms of physical appearance, clothing is the joker you get to play every day.

Get the outfit right, and you stand out. Get it wrong, and you also stand out but for all the wrong reasons. You might attract looks of mockery, pity and even contempt – all before you've even opened your mouth.

In the words of French fashion icon Coco Chanel: "Dress shabbily and they remember the dress; dress impeccably and they remember the woman."[1]

Whether you're dressed for a job interview, a social event or a quick visit to the corner shop, you cannot escape the message your attire sends out. It's a form of self-expression, whether it's a sexy black number, a casual outfit or a pair of faded jeans. To paraphrase the 17th-century French philosopher René Descartes: I dress; therefore I am.

How did you feel the last time you put on a smart, well-tailored business suit, all perfectly accessorised and coordinated with a cotton shirt and leather shoes? Probably powerful, confident and ready to take on the world.

How did you feel the last time you slipped into a flattering, figure-hugging dress, your legs beautifully accentuated by elegant heels, your hair perfectly styled and your neck adorned with a tasteful piece of jewellery? Probably sexy, desirable and confident in your ability to turn heads.

Despite the growing acceptance of more casual attire, both in business and social settings, formal dress still makes a powerful statement. It communicates professionalism, trustworthiness and leadership.[2] As Oscar Wilde said: "You can never be overdressed or overeducated."[3]

The psychology of dress is a well-documented field of study.[4] Our clothing doesn't just protect us from the elements or cover up our modesty; it also improves our mood and self-esteem. It can even reduce the risk of depression. Looking and feeling your best can positively affect your stride and posture. It can influence the impression people have of you and make them more open to engaging with you. Even the colour of your clothes affects your mood and how others perceive you. For example, warm colours like red, orange and yellow evoke very different emotions compared with cool colours like blue, purple or green.[5]

In the workplace, research shows that dressing well makes you perform better and enhances people's perception of you.[6] Then again, this is just common sense. Imagine coming straight out of the gym, all sweaty in your gym clothes, and going into a critical client meeting. How competent do you reckon you'll feel? How seriously do you think you'll be taken?

Facebook chief Mark Zuckerberg might get away with his signature jeans and grey T-shirt at work because he's the boss there. But even he dons a suit and tie when testifying before

Congress. The power dynamic there is different, and a suit sends out the right signal. He may be rich, but he's not stupid. It's also why defendants on trial are advised by their lawyers to dress neatly, and preferably formally. It's a sign of respect for both the judge and the jury, who potentially hold a defendant's life in their hands. Expert witnesses, such as doctors and ballistics specialists, also dress formally because it lends credibility to their testimony.[7]

What kind of statement do you make when you dress up? What are the non-verbal cues that your clothing projects? Is it perhaps how smart you are? How much you earn? Your social status?

There are endless fashion options to play around with, from style, cut and fabric to colour, pattern and accessories.[8] Do you want to look mature, formal and professional? Or do you prefer young, casual and edgy? Are you somebody brand-conscious who must be seen in Burberry, Gucci or Hugo Boss? Or are you happy buying your clothes at Marks & Spencer, Zara or H&M? Is your watch a Rolex or a Swatch? How about your shoes? Leather or canvas? Flats or something with a bit of heel?

Deciding what to wear each morning can take time, especially if you're a high-profile person in the public eye. It's one reason presidents, prime ministers and CEOs tend to wear the same basic cut and colour; they have enough decisions to make every day without also having to worry about how to dress. Steve Jobs wore blue jeans and a black turtleneck;[9] Barack Obama's suits were always blue or grey;[10] French president Emmanuel Macron always wears the same off-the-shelf suit in different shades of blue.[11]

When it comes to getting ready, whether for work or a social occasion, women take far more time than men.[12] Looking good and attractive matters far more to them. Also, they're more sensitive to mood, colour and style,[13] so it takes longer to find the appropriate outfit in a closet that might have a bewildering array of jackets, tops, blouses, scarves, pants, dresses, skirts and shoes – not to mention earrings, jewellery, handbags and accessories. Not for nothing do some women say that getting ready is half the fun.

We men are more practical – sometimes depressingly so. We have far fewer outfits in our closet, dress more for comfort and practicality (even when we want to look good) and can get ready in a fraction of the time. However, we may still have to field the inevitable question from our better half: "You're not wearing *that* again, are you?!" Unlike women, who go out of their way to have a distinct and unique look, we men are quite happy to blend in with our peers in our lookalike suits. Whether in the workplace, at weddings or at the Oscars, it's always the women who stand out.

Men also have a relatively easy ride when they dress up because they only have to be men; they don't need to project any feminine qualities.

Women, on the other hand, may also have to look authoritative – for example, in the workplace or when doing a media interview – and that's a traditionally masculine quality. It can be a tough balancing act, as one study showed. If a woman comes across as too soft and feminine (with hair loose and lots of skin showing, for example), she doesn't project the masculine attributes of dominance and expertise; if she looks too hard and masculine (for instance, wearing a pantsuit with her hair severely tied up), she doesn't project the feminine attributes of friendliness and likeability.[14] Trying to straddle these extremes can leave modern professional women in a no-win situation.

Then again, perhaps you don't go in for all this fashion nonsense, and you reckon it's a big capitalist plot to make people spend money. We should all be judged for who we really are deep down, and not for such superficialities as the clothes on our back. So, you deliberately dress down, going for plain and sustainable, even if it means buying second-hand. However, even this makes a statement. You're still sending a message out into the world – and probably not a very flattering one – and people will judge you accordingly.

When you choose your clothes in the morning, you also choose your sartorial stereotype for the day.

8

Demeanour

D EMEANOUR IS YOUR OUTWARD behaviour or bearing, or how you conduct yourself in any given moment. It includes body language, facial expression and eye contact. Demeanour is critical in how you are stereotyped.

For example, you can have a friendly, shy or hostile demeanour. People may like you; they may be coolly indifferent; or they may be afraid. Your demeanour is the first real indication of the kind of person you are.

Demeanour can be the great leveller, compensating for any positive physical attributes you may be lacking. Even a tall, handsome man won't make much of an impression if he is rude and overbearing. An attractive woman with a great figure will just alienate those around her if she's got a bad attitude.

A rule of thumb is that the friendlier your demeanour, the better people respond to you,[1] whether you're out shopping, at work or ordering in a restaurant. The more antagonistic you are – even if it's for good reason – the less cooperative they will be. And walking around with a chip on your shoulder is perhaps the worst demeanour of all.

Of course, there's a cultural dimension to this, too. In the US and many African countries, for example, people are generally outwardly friendly and smile a lot, even at strangers. In Germany and other northern European countries, on the other hand, such outward signs of friendliness are rare, and tourists may even find the natives "cold". In his hugely entertaining book, *The Almost Nearly Perfect People: Behind the Myth of the Scandinavian Utopia*, travel writer Michael Booth discovers a distinct taciturnity, aloofness and reluctance to engage in chit-chat in public. In Sweden, his attempts to break through people's defences with deliberately outrageous behaviour – such as noisily eating crisps and slurping Coke in the hushed atmosphere of a museum – meet with little success.[2] You'll also find this seemingly standoffish behaviour in certain Asian countries, where strong emotions tend not to be displayed publicly.

In business, they sometimes say it's good to be hard and stern; being friendly apparently makes you come across as weak, especially in negotiations. I don't buy that; it's firmness and resolve that matter. Nobody ever thundered and blustered their way to a good deal. If anything, courtesy and respect can disarm your adversary and get them to drop their guard. Just ask Lieutenant Columbo, the shrewd TV detective who always unmasks the murderer in the end because they take his courteous demeanour and dishevelled appearance for a lack of intelligence.[3]

Here's an example of how demeanour may well have kept me out of jail after an encounter with two American police officers in Washington DC during my first visit to the US in 1991.

Late one afternoon, with daylight fading fast, I found myself strolling near the US Capitol building, where President George Bush Sr was just a few hours away from giving his annual State of the Union address. It was a tense time worldwide. The Gulf War – also known as Operation Desert Storm – was raging in response to the Iraqi invasion of Kuwait, and the US was the major military force during the operation. Security was tight wherever the president went.

But I was in tourist mode. I merrily clicked away with my camera, not noticing the increasingly suspicious stares of a couple of cops patrolling nearby.

The two gun-toting policemen stopped me. Awkwardly, but politely, they asked me if they could have a look at the camera. Sure, I said, understanding their concern and seeing how suspicious I must have looked.

"We might have to confiscate your film, sir."

"Oh? In that case, I'd like my pictures developed and handed back to me."

He frowned: this clearly wasn't the reaction he had been expecting. He asked me for some ID. Sorry, I left it at my hotel, but here's the number – feel free to call. He stepped to one side, spoke into his walkie-talkie and got someone to check me out. Meanwhile, I chatted amiably with his young partner, who told me how the war had made them nervous and edgy. He was curious about South Africa and asked me about the evolving political situation there. Eventually, sensing that my behaviour didn't fit that of a terrorist casing the joint for a bomb attack, they both apologised, returned my camera and cheerfully waved goodbye.

"Enjoy the rest of your stay."

"And carry your passport next time!"

At no time during the encounter did I feel concerned or worried. With no prior experience of the American police, I had no reason to believe they would be anything other than courteous and professional. After all, aren't the cops the good guys? Simplistic, and perhaps even naïve, but that was the image I had internalised growing up watching American cop series on television. This encounter merely confirmed it. Of course, that was a long time ago, and I have no idea if it would still play out in the same way today.

It was a classic illustration of stereotyping in action. They had sized me up as a well-dressed, clueless tourist and treated me accordingly. I had sized them up as a couple of decent cops just doing their job and treated them accordingly. I had read their faces and they had read mine. No threat on either side. Human nature took over after that. Who knows how the encounter might have turned out if they had been pushy and aggressive, or I had been indignant and self-righteous?

In the courtroom, the demeanour of a witness giving testimony can sometimes be an indication of how truthful they are. Tell-tale signs are facial expression, eye contact and fidgeting. In 2020, at the height of the Covid-19 pandemic when faces were covered for health reasons, a San Francisco state judge ruled that witnesses giving testimony had to wear transparent face-masks so that jurors could read their facial expressions and assess their credibility.[4]

In a particularly fascinating paper titled "Courtroom Demeanour: The Theater of the Courtroom", published in the *Minnesota Law Review*, the author argues that the courtroom is not a mere laboratory where testimony and information are dispassionately processed by an unbiased jury. Rather, it is a theatre in which a human drama plays out featuring many different parties – the judge, the jury, the defendant, witnesses, lawyers and even the gallery.[5]

One could make a similar argument for that other theatre of demeanour – the job interview. It is by no means a neutral, dispassionate evaluation of skills and experience by an unbiased interviewer. As recruitment experts never fail to emphasise, it's also about how you come across. Your posture, voice, body language and facial expression – even the firmness of your handshake – are all an indication of the kind of person you are.[6] For example, an upbeat attitude of genuine warmth and quiet confidence speaks volumes about you as a prospective colleague. In a competitive job market, similar-looking résumés are a dime a dozen, and one MBA looks pretty much like the next; but there's only one you – and you've been a lifetime in the making.

Your demeanour is like a fingerprint. It is a critical element of the stereotype you project in the world.

9
Voice

THERE'S A FORM OF stereotyping we engage in almost every day when we're on the phone speaking to somebody we don't know. It's called voice-stereotyping – also known as linguistic profiling – and it involves using auditory cues to get an idea of what a person is like.[1]

We usually know within seconds whether we are talking to, say, a young woman, a middle-aged man or a five-year-old child. A female voice has a distinctly higher, almost lyrical pitch, whereas a male voice is lower and deeper. A child's voice is particularly high but will deepen as they mature. Both men and women sound different as they get older.

Then there's accent, tone of voice and how loudly or softly they speak. A wide vocabulary, good grammar and proper pronunciation indicate a good command of language. On the other hand, constant use of slang, "like" and "y'know", for example, suggests poor communication skills. Before you know it, you've got a handle on the person's education level and social class. You can even pick up on their mood: if they're anxious or stressed, their voice may sound scratchy and uneven, whereas a calm voice is smooth and well-modulated.

If you like the voice, you will probably like the person behind it, too – that's the halo effect in action. Studies show that a person's voice reveals everything from trustworthiness and leadership to height and even fertility (in women).[2] It also reveals aspects of one's personality – for example, a deep voice is associated with being dominant and extroverted.[3]

People with an attractive voice enjoy a tremendous stereotype advantage in life. They may go on to become voiceover artists, narrating advertisements, documentaries and audiobooks.

Perhaps the most famous voice of the past few decades has been that of American actor James Earl Jones.[4] His rich, resonant tones, coupled with superb enunciation and delivery, lent gravel and gravitas to the countless roles he played, not just on screen, but also on the stage doing Shakespeare. Jones was the iconic voice behind the villain Darth Vader in *Star Wars* and the wise Mufasa in *The Lion King.* Another million-dollar voice – literally, if his fees are any indication – is that of veteran Hollywood actor Morgan Freeman. His deep, distinctive vocal tone is an industry unto itself and has made him a sought-after narrator.[5]

Another attribute that's easy to spot in a voice is ethnicity. Here in South Africa where I live, I can tell with near certainty which of our four official population groups a person comes from: black, white, Indian or coloured (mixed race). You can probably do the same in your country, because ethnic and regional differences are usually very distinct. For example, it's a rare British person who can't tell someone from Yorkshire or Liverpool in the north from someone from Sussex or Berkshire in the south.

In the US, people from southern states like Texas and Louisiana speak very differently from those in New England states like Vermont and New Hampshire. Black Americans sound particularly distinctive. They may speak a non-standard form of English called African-American Vernacular English, especially when they're together in a non-professional set-ting.[6] This dialect comes with its own distinctive grammar and speech sounds. In a study on the phenomenon of "sounding black", we learn that listeners can identify a black voice with considerable accuracy within seconds, sometimes after just a single word.[7]

This seems impressive, but I'm pretty sure that black listeners could identify a white voice with similar accuracy. It's not rocket science. People exposed to different ethnicities soon develop a keen ear for their distinctive ways of speaking.

Linguistic profiling is even recognised as legitimate testimony in a court of law.[8] This is because crimes are often committed by people whose faces are covered or obscured by darkness, which of course makes identification problematic. Obscene or threatening phone calls, for example, would be impossible to investigate without linguistic profiling. A judge may rule that it's okay to testify to what a person sounded like – for example: male or female, or white or black. There are well-known court cases in which people have been convicted based on such testimony.[9]

We know from music that there are six basic types of voice: bass, baritone and tenor in men; and contralto, mezzo-soprano and soprano in women.[10] Men occupy the lower ranges because of thicker and longer vocal cords, which develop during adolescence because of testosterone. The lower, deeper male voice evokes authority, dominance and confidence. This is why certain women in business and politics deepen their voice, often with the help of a professional voice coach; former British prime minister Margaret Thatcher was a note-worthy example.[11] The higher-pitched female voice, which is also clearer and more distinct, evokes warmth, kindness and friendliness.[12]

These male/female differences become relevant for the recording of voiceovers for videos, advertisements and public announcements. Voiceover professionals typically recommend the use of a male voice for a forceful message and a female voice for a reassuring message.[13] Popular voice assistants like Alexa (Amazon) and Siri (Apple) are all female. The vocal style also matters, some common ones being warm, likeable, reassuring, trustworthy and thoughtful.[14]

At my health club in Johannesburg, the friendly female voice on the PA system reminding people to wipe down the exercise equipment after use was recently replaced by a more emphatic and forceful male voice. Personally, I find it much more effective in getting people to comply.

Even in face-to-face encounters with other people, the voice still carries immense power in shaping how we judge them.

On 28 August 1963, black civil-rights leader Martin Luther King Jr. gave his famous "I have a dream" speech to a quarter of a million people from the steps of the Lincoln Memorial in Washington DC.[15] Delivered in a deep, rich and resonant voice, it was one of the most iconic speeches in US history. It moved an entire nation and marked the beginning of equal rights and freedoms for black people. King's masterful oratory skills notwithstanding, it is doubtful whether the speech would have had the same impact if it had been delivered in a soft, nasal, high-pitched voice.

Ultimately, our voice is what connects us to others. Until we open our mouths to speak, we are just a tantalising package of flesh and blood that hasn't yet come alive – like a beautifully wrapped present whose contents have yet to be revealed.

10

Accent

THE ENGLISH TEACHER ASKS the student from India to construct a sentence using the words "defence", "defeat" and "detail". He answers: "De dog jumps over de fence; first de feet and den de tail."

"I'm going to lie on ze bitch," says the Frenchman. Of course, he means "the beach".

Making fun of accents is a staple of stand-up comedy, and it's a rare comedian who doesn't rip off the way others speak. There are many amusing videos online showing various nationalities – particularly the French – comically mangling English words.[1] Other nationalities in turn make fun of English-speakers trying to pronounce words from their respective languages.

Accents are mocked and parodied within countries, too. In the US, it's the Southern accent; in England, the Yorkshire accent; and in Germany, the Bavarian accent. These accents deviate so strongly from what is considered the norm that they provoke mirth, pity and even disdain. People from these regions may soften their accent or drop it altogether, especially when looking for work.[2]

Accents are fertile ground for stereotyping because of what they evoke.

A standard accent generally evokes power, education and influence. It is dominant in gleaming capital cities inhabited by clever people doing business deals, lecturing at universities and reading the news on television. A regional accent, on the other hand, might evoke simplicity, manual labour and traditional values, and is more likely to be found in the countryside or on farms. City people often sound smooth and mellifluous; countryfolk may sound harsh and guttural, or twangy with a lazy drawl. Think Washington DC versus the American south; London versus the rural north of England; or Paris versus Marseille. This linguistic divide is often parodied in movies about the smooth city slicker who finds himself stuck in a small town in the middle of nowhere and battles to understand the locals.

A strong regional accent is a heavy burden to carry in the job market. A British study found that people were less likely to want to be represented in court by a barrister with a strong regional accent, instead preferring one with a standard or upper-class accent.[3] This "accentism", or accent-discrimination, is a concern in many countries.[4] In France, for example, it is unlawful to discriminate against regional accents, and guilty parties can face up to three years in jail and a fine of €45 000.[5] Many of the country's regional accents are strongly associated with simplicity, rural life and a lack of education, and this doesn't always play well in business, politics and the media.[6]

No accent is ever neutral; it always says something about the person speaking it.[7]

For example, English spoken with a Russian accent doesn't evoke the same associations as English spoken with, say, a French accent. The two countries are simply too far apart in terms of their reputation and impact on popular culture. When was the last time you watched a Russian movie, dined in a Russian restaurant or bought something with a "Made in

Russia" sticker on it? But chances are you've recently watched a French movie, eaten in a French restaurant or bought French perfume; you may even drive a French car. Paris is the city of love, gastronomy and the Eiffel Tower; Moscow conjures up images of hardship, snow and sub-zero temperatures. There are 485 movie titles containing the word "Paris" (for example, *To Paris with Love*, *An American in Paris* and *Last Tango in Paris*), but just 72 with the word "Moscow".[8] Don't hold your breath for a Netflix series called *Emily in Moscow*. Associations are anything but trivial; scratch the surface of any stereotype and you'll eventually find one. So, everything that France represents rubs off favourably on a French person speaking English.

The standard British accent also enjoys a positive reputation, especially in the US, where it is associated with sophistication, class and intelligence[9] – think *Downton Abbey*. Britons in America know this and have a huge advantage in the workplace and on the dating front. Black Britons also benefit from this accent advantage, which immediately marks them out as different from black Americans.[10] At the other extreme, an accent from a developing or low-status country is usually judged less favourably, even though the speaker may be intelligent, cultivated and successful. That's because such countries – especially in Africa and South America – don't evoke many positive associations. The little we do know about them comes from sensationalised media reports of war, famine, drugs, corruption, failed economies and state incompetence.

Quite apart from what an accent evokes, there's the more practical matter of what it sounds like. A non-standard accent – whether regional or foreign – can be difficult to understand, research shows.[11] The enunciation, intonation and pronunciation are all different, so the brain must work harder to decode it. One study has shown that infants and young children prefer native accents to foreign accents, even before they themselves have learned to speak.[12] A person who speaks in a particularly strong foreign accent may even be perceived as less credible and trustworthy.[13] This is something you might have noticed online if you've ever watched a video narrated in an accent you aren't used to.

Standard German (High German, or *Hochdeutsch*[14]) sounds smooth and pure, and is easier to understand than the German spoken in Austria. The German spoken in Switzerland is even further off the scale in terms of accent, and Germans themselves may struggle to understand it.

French-speakers have a similar problem with the French spoken in Québec, Canada, and often can't understand it on television without subtitles. In my first year at university in France, my fellow French students and I encountered a lively group of girls visiting from Québec. They were the subject of much good-natured teasing because of their strange accent, which just didn't come across as, well, "proper".

Accent discrimination is viewed mostly through the lens of being treated unfairly, but the opposite is also true. Having the "right" accent can open doors and make people favourably disposed towards you. No matter your native language, you will always be impressed by someone who speaks it well.

The hit movie from my childhood years, *My Fair Lady*, remains to this day the quintessential illustration of this. A professor who is an expert in phonetics takes a poor London flower-seller with a Cockney accent and teaches her to speak so well that she is taken for a duchess at an embassy ball.[15]

You may reasonably object that adopting a posh accent just to impress others is somehow fake and inauthentic. Perhaps, but then so is dressing up smartly for a job interview or a date – it's just a matter of degree.

11

Name

"**W**HAT'S IN A NAME?**" asks Juliet in the famous balcony scene in Shakespeare's *Romeo and Juliet*. "That which we call a rose, by any other word would smell as sweet. So, Romeo would – were he not Romeo called – retain that dear perfection which he owes without that title."[1]

Well, Juliet clearly wasn't aware of the hidden meaning of names.

If a modern-day Romeo applied for a job, he'd immediately be labelled as Italian – which, depending on the context, is not always flattering. Worse, Romeo is a synonym for the kind of philandering Lothario (another Italian word) you would not want to see hanging around your daughter – as in: "Who's the Romeo chatting up the girls at the bar?"

Names come pre-loaded with information about gender, class, background, education, ethnicity and much more.

Names like Sandy, Debbie or Roxie send out a very different message than, say, Catherine, Victoria or Juliet. Elizabeth Carrington says class in a way that Barbie Tripper does not. Cameron Wendell-Holmes speaks old money far better than, say, Rick Smith. Then there are names that mark their owners out ethnically, such as Ariel or Leah (Jewish), Hassan and Fatima (Arab), or Jamal and Shanice (African American).

These subtleties are well understood by novelists and screenwriters, who face the challenge of choosing the right names for their characters. For example, the villain should have a name that evokes a bad guy and not some wimpy milquetoast; the seductive *femme fatale* should have a name that gels with her predatory sexual nature rather than the sunny disposition of the girl next door. There are even name-generator websites that spit out appropriate names for characters depending on gender, age, personality and their role in the story.[2]

Research has demonstrated that when people within a given culture are shown a random face and given a handful of names, they pick the right name with an accuracy greater than chance. Machine-learning algorithms do it with even greater accuracy.[3] When you get an email from, say, a Molly, she looks different in your mind from a Heather or an Annabelle. I recently exchanged emails with a Theo who was organising a book event for me. A guy, right? Wrong. Theo was Theodora, a girl's name. So much for first impressions.

That said, gender does trigger specific associations in our minds. A man's name is typically associated with masculine attributes such as strength, power and aggression, whereas a woman's name is typically associated with feminine attributes such as empathy, likeability and agreeableness. A study on the impact of hurricanes, featured in the journal *Proceedings of the National Academy of Sciences*, found that hurricanes carrying a woman's name caused significantly more deaths than those carrying a man's name. Apparently, female-named hurricanes were perceived to be less deadly because of the less threatening attributes associated with femininity. Consequently, people took less protective action and were less likely to evacuate, resulting in more casualties.[4] In other words, a

Hurricane Alexander is likely to be taken more seriously than, say, a Hurricane Emily.

Clearly, a name is not neutral. It colours your perception of the person behind it.

This is not exactly news in the corporate sector, where the naming of products (and companies) is big business.[5] It requires the services of brand consultancies, research organisations and even linguists. A name must be catchy and easy to say; it must have the right personality; and it must travel well and evoke positive associations.

So, if you're selling a food-related product, a French-sounding name might work because of that country's culinary reputation. A good example is the fresh-food-and-sandwich chain Pret (from *prêt-à-manger*, which literally means "ready to eat"). It evokes a certain culinary sophistication that a name like, say, Joe's Sandwich Joint would not. If you're into anything automotive, it wouldn't hurt to borrow from German because of that country's reputation for great cars. There's a company in Johannesburg that specialises in the repair and servicing of Mercedes-Benz vehicles; it's called German Autohaus (*Haus* in German means "house"). Very clever.

So much for positive associations; what about negative ones?

After two fatal crashes in 2018 and 2019 of the just-unveiled Boeing 737 MAX and its worldwide grounding for more than a year, the name no longer had a positive association in the minds of the flying public and potential airline customers. Boeing quietly started dropping the word "MAX" in official announcements, referring to the plane simply as the 737-8. But it never really caught on. Just as well, because Boeing bounced back, fixed the problem and now has a bulging order book of more than 4 000 units.[6] However, early in 2024, a MAX door panel blew out in flight, and the reliability of the plane was once again called into question.[7] Time will tell whether the MAX rides out the storm or whether it becomes the Edsel of aviation – an unflattering reference to the Ford Edsel of the late 1950s, a much-hyped model that went on to become a spectacular commercial failure.[8]

Name discrimination has been the subject of many studies, from the US, England and Belgium to Peru, China and Australia.[9] It typically involves forming two groups of applicants with distinctly different kinds of names – say, black-sounding names versus white-sounding names, or city names versus regional names. The objective is to establish how the two groups are treated in real-life situations, such as applying for a job or renting an apartment.

In every single case, there is name discrimination. For example, men are preferred over women for certain occupations, and vice-versa; candidates with traditional names have an edge over those with less common regional names; and local applicants are preferred to those with foreign-sounding names. This discrimination happens both across and within ethnicities, cultures and even genders. In other words, whites may discriminate against other whites; blacks may discriminate against other blacks; and women may discriminate against other women.

This isn't surprising. If different names evoke different associations – and they do – then it is only logical that they should be perceived differently. Recruiters and landlords, who must often sift through huge volumes of applications, have neither the time nor the inclination to delve into the life circumstances of every single applicant; nor can they bring all of them in for an interview. There are only so many hours in the day, and only so much you can do to be fair. Name-stereotyping is inevitable, and this may well influence the outcome.

To counter that, certain companies resort to blind hiring, which is the practice of using résumés that have been stripped of not just the candidate's name but also their age, gender, address and anything that might trigger bias.[10] The idea is to focus on a candidate's skills and nothing else. But when was the last time you saw a disembodied set of skills walking around the office? Ultimately, you hire a person, not a résumé. The jury is still out on the effectiveness of blind hiring. Its proponents say it can improve diversity; its detractors say it can bring in employees who are a bad cultural fit with the values of the organisation.[11]

Meanwhile, your name will continue to mark you out in life. Of course, if you don't like it, you can always change it. Many people do. Perhaps the name is too long, too difficult to pronounce or too close to that of a notorious public figure. Changes are particularly common in music and showbiz, where artists may prefer a stage name. Examples are Elton John (Reginald Kenneth Dwight), Alicia Keys (Alicia Cook) and Tom Cruise (Thomas Cruise Mapother IV).

Nevertheless, once people get to know you, your name becomes less of an issue. After all, a man called Barack Obama was elected US president – twice.

12
Job

YOU'RE AT A SOCIAL event among people you don't know. Sooner or later, someone asks you what you do.

"I'm an architect. Commercial high rises, mainly."

"Fascinating! What are some of the buildings you've designed?"

"I'm an airline pilot."

"Oh, wow – I wish I could jet around the world every day and be paid for it!"

"I'm a social worker."

"Oh? That's interesting..."

Okay, it's just a thought-experiment, but you get the picture. Your line of work immediately labels you, revealing your status in society and how much money you make. As the humorous poet Ogden Nash observed, people who work sitting down get paid more than people who work standing up.[1]

Your job may even indicate which way you lean politically. Despite much overlap, liberals (left-leaning) are more likely to be found in creative professions such as music, movie scriptwriting and newspaper editing, while conservatives (right-leaning) are more likely to be surgeons, bankers and engineers. An oft-cited reason is that conservatives prefer structure and order, whereas liberals are more open to ambiguity and change.[2]

Your profession also speaks to how smart you are. IQ (intelligence quotient), a score derived from a set of standardised tests, is closely associated with the ability to pursue certain fields of study and succeed in certain lines of work.[3] Studies have shown that IQ is a reliable predictor of career success, and perhaps even the most important one.[4]

The cognitive and reasoning ability needed to work as, say, a nuclear physicist, corporate lawyer or aerospace engineer is very different from that required in a more manual, repetitive job like construction worker, insurance-claims manager or dental assistant. Even the US military puts applicants through a battery of general intelligence tests and does not recruit those with very low scores.[5]

At the other end of the intelligence scale, squarely in genius territory, are people with an IQ above 130 – less than 2% of the population.[6] Well-known names said to lie beyond this threshold are business icons like Elon Musk, Jeff Bezos, Bill Gates and Mark Zuckerberg[7] – and the late Steve Jobs, co-founder of Apple, who apparently had an IQ of around 160.[8]

Are we born intelligent, or do we become it? Evidence suggests it's both.

According to an article in *New Scientist*, hundreds of studies have shown that intelligence is at least to some degree hereditary. About 50% of the difference in intelligence between people is estimated to be genetic, with the rest coming from environmental factors.[9] A 20-year-long study of 245 children adopted at birth showed that their IQ bore little correlation with that of their adopted parents but was very strongly correlated with that of their biological parents.[10]

Your job doesn't just speak to your intelligence; it also speaks to your status. According to an American survey, some jobs are seen as contributing more to society and are associated with factors such as a higher level of education, the ability to inspire trust, and even strength and courage. Topping the list of the most-respected professions are doctors, scientists, farmers, firefighters and teachers; at the bottom are social-media influencers, reality-TV stars and politicians.[11] In another survey, conducted in 35 countries, doctors topped the list, followed by lawyers and engineers.[12]

Your job is a big stereotype factor when it comes to dating, especially if you're a man. A study involving 1.8 million online daters from 24 countries found that women were more likely to date successful, highly educated men who earn a lot.[13]

Extensive research across many different cultures shows that women rate factors like ambition and industriousness in a prospective partner very highly.[14] A man needs to be a good financial prospect with a certain socio-economic status. His job must allow him to provide a home, security and material comfort – and eventually to raise a family. Given the obvious economic cost[15] to women of having to take time out of their lives – often at the peak of their career – to have children and raise them, it seems reasonable that they would want a degree of material security. A woman might overlook a man's line of work for a casual fling, but not when it comes to a relationship. In a survey by a dating service, 75% of women said they were unlikely to date an unemployed man.[16]

In the social sciences, this is known as hypergamy.[17] Women are hypergamous – that is, they date and marry across and up status hierarchies. Men, on the other hand, date and marry across and down. They don't mind if a woman is less successful than they are, so long as she is attractive first and foremost, as well as loving, kind and supportive – the so-called traditional feminine virtues. When it comes to objectification – the act of reducing someone to the status of a mere object – men are objects of success to women, while women are objects of beauty to men. It's why you're more likely to see an attractive woman married to a successful, plain-looking man than an attractive man married to a successful, plain-looking woman.

If the huge volume of online debate on the issue is anything to go by, men don't necessarily want an independent, successful woman who earns more than them. It strips away their basic instinctual need to provide and protect, leaving them without a primary role in the relationship.[18] Successful women can also come across as intimidating and masculine, which clashes with the femininity and agreeableness that men generally desire.[19]

In any event, the jobs that men and women find appealing in each other differ markedly. The dating site Tinder has released several rankings in recent years of the most desirable job titles in online dating.[20] Although choices vary from country to country to reflect cultural and social differences, women who are nurses, teachers or flight attendants generally attract much male interest, while men who are firefighters, engineers or pilots are appealing to women.

Clearly, your line of work plays a big role in the way you are stereotyped.

13

Blondes

A BLONDE IS STUCK at the roadside after her Porsche breaks down. Another blonde, also driving a Porsche, pulls alongside to lend a hand.

"What's the matter?"

"It just died on me."

"Let me have a look inside."

The stranded blonde pops the hood of her Porsche, then steps back in horror.

"There's no engine!"

"Don't fret, honey – I've got a spare in the back of mine."

This classic joke plays on the stereotypical image of the sweet, attractive blonde who also happens to be cerebrally challenged. Twisting the knife even further, it is clearly a case of the blonde leading the blonde. Now try changing the protagonists to two brunettes. It would not be even remotely funny. What brunette would be that stupid?

The term "dumb blonde" is so entrenched in the English language that it hardly requires explanation. It is said to have originated in an 18th-century satirical French play in which a blonde courtesan would pause markedly before speaking, in the process appearing both beautiful and stupid.[1]

To be blonde and attractive is clearly a mixed blessing on the stereotype front. On the one hand, you enjoy all the advantages of great looks; on the other, you're thought to be a touch ditzy and missing a few neurons upstairs.

This pejorative image has been reinforced in popular culture for decades in comic strips, books and movies.[2] The smart female character is almost always dark-haired and gets by on her wits. The blonde female character, on the other hand, coasts effortlessly through the plot on her looks. The assumption of limited intelligence goes to the heart of the hit movie *Legally Blonde*, in which Elle Woods (played by Reese Witherspoon) goes to Harvard Law School and must battle the perception that there's not much grey matter behind her pretty face, attractive figure and bubbly personality.[3]

The English language abounds with terms such as "blondes have more fun", "gentlemen prefer blondes" and, of course, "blonde bombshell" – the latter epitomised by Hollywood actress Marilyn Monroe, one of the most popular sex-symbols of the 20th century.[4]

There's clearly envy tied up in the stereotype of the dumb blonde. If she's so attractive, the logic goes, then she must be lacking something. Nature couldn't have blessed her with both blond hair *and* intelligence.

In any event, it hasn't stopped millions of people around the world from dyeing their hair blond; imitation is the sincerest form of flattery.

Women dye their hair blond; men dye their hair blond. Straight people dye their hair blond; gay people dye their hair blond. Black people dye their hair blond; Japanese people dye their hair blond. Pampered pooches are dyed blond by their (presumably) blond owners. The whole world covets this seemingly magical hair colour, which is so rare that it occurs naturally in barely 2% of the world's population.[5]

The history of blond hair is a rich one.[6] In Roman times, lightening the hair or wearing a blond wig was a popular way of standing out from the dark-haired populace; in medieval Europe, artwork of Eve sometimes showed her with long, blond hair framing her nude body; in the 20th century, Adolf Hitler tried to make blond a symbol of racial purity – which is a bit rich, given that he himself wasn't blond. Over millennia, blond has had a schizophrenic existence, being associated with innocence, love and purity as well as sexual looseness, immorality and feminine stupidity. But it has stubbornly maintained its attraction as a hair colour of choice.[7]

There are dozens of different shades of blond in a global hair-colour market worth more than $20 billion.[8] There's ash blond, platinum blond, sandy blond, strawberry blond, honey blond and many more. There's even Hitchcock blond, a reference to legendary filmmaker Alfred Hitchcock's tendency to cast blonde women in his films, as he believed that the audience would be least likely to suspect them.

Why do people dye their hair blond? Because it makes them feel better about themselves in some weird, inexplicable way. Joanna Pitman, author of *On Blondes*, found out for herself when she dyed her hair blond. In an article in *The Guardian* titled "To dye for", she says: "I feel as if I'm younger, funnier. I smile more ... It's like how you behave when it's sunny rather than when it's dull and drizzly."[9]

It would seem as if blond is not so much a hair colour as a psychology.[10] Even British celebrity chef Nigella Lawson – already a sex-symbol to millions of men and hardly in need of a makeover – briefly went blonde, generating a flurry of news commentary.

A recurring theme among women who dye their hair blond is that they come across as more attractive, carefree and fun-loving, which clearly plays into the prevailing stereotype. They are noticed more and get asked out more. On the downside, however, it can harm their career prospects. Research shows that blondes are turned down more often than equally qualified brunettes for the same job, particularly at managerial level. Even when they are employed in a similar position, they earn less than their dark-haired counterparts.[11] There have been reports of blondes dyeing their hair a darker colour to be taken more seriously in the workplace.[12] One blonde Silicon Valley CEO, keen to de-sexualise her appearance, went even further by ditching her heels, wearing loose-fitting clothes and swapping her contact lenses for spectacles.[13]

However, this hasn't stopped blonde women – both natural and with dyed hair – from becoming successful leaders in business and politics. According to findings by two business-school researchers, some 48% of female CEOs at S&P 500 companies and 35% of female senators are blonde.[14] The explanation offered for this seemingly paradoxical statistic is that the attractiveness and femininity associated with being blonde disarms their mostly male colleagues and allows them to get away with the authority required by their position. Translation: men find blonde women less intimidating.

There is no evidence that blondes are inherently less smart than brunettes; indeed, one study suggests the opposite may be true.[15] Blondes are scientists, engineers, pilots, astronauts, doctors and everything in between. Nevertheless, the dumb-blonde stereotype remains stubbornly anchored in the public consciousness. If stereotype accuracy has one glaring exception, then this must surely be it.

To their credit, blondes are remarkably tolerant of the stereotype. They don't take to the streets waving placards and complaining about "blondism". Sensitivity to the special needs of blondes is not an element of diversity training. You can't always tell an ethnic joke or a religious joke, but you can tell a blonde joke – even when blondes are present. In fact, blondes are often the first to parody themselves, as a delightfully irreverent online video titled *12 Everyday Problems of Blonde Girls* shows.[16] Country singer Dolly Parton famously said: "I'm not offended by all the dumb-blonde jokes because I know I'm not dumb ... and I also know I'm not blonde."[17]

Of course, blonde discrimination is not in the same league as ethnic discrimination. Nevertheless, in these hyper-sensitive days of kneejerk offence-taking, it is a mature attitude that speaks to a solid sense of self among the species.

14

Nationality

H EAVEN IS WHERE THE police are British, the chefs French, the mechanics German, the lovers Italian and everything is organised by the Swiss.

Hell is where the police are German, the lovers Swiss, the mechanics French, the chefs British and everything is organised by the Italians.

I first heard this joke at high school, some fifty years ago. It has held up well because the underlying stereotypes are still broadly true. The French are culinary masters in the kitchen; the Germans are renowned for superior engineering; and in Switzerland, well, everything just functions like clockwork.

We talk about British fair play, French flair and German engineering. These terms are so entrenched in everyday language that they don't even require explanation.

On the other hand, nobody speaks of German fair play, British flair or French engineering. That would prompt much head-scratching and perhaps even a laugh. It doesn't mean that fair play is alien to Germans, the British have no flair or French engineering is sub-standard. It's just that these are not the most dominant national characteristics that spring to mind when we think of these places.

National stereotypes aren't just good for a laugh; they are also the first superficial insight into other cultures.[1] I learned this growing up in Zambia in the 1970s, where my friends, teachers and university lecturers came from all over the world. British people were funny and self-deprecating; Americans were loud and brash; Canadians were polite and unpretentious; Indians were studious and hard-working – and good at maths; Zambians were friendly and helpful; and the French were suave and sophisticated. Of course, they were not *just* these things, but that's what stood out.

National differences matter in business, and being culturally illiterate is not good for the bottom line. Executives about to take up a position in a new country often attend specialised workshops to prepare themselves for the culture shock they will encounter.

Take business lunches. If you're American, British or even German, a business lunch means just that – you're going to do business over lunch. How literal! You generally don't linger over pointless conversation or, heaven forbid, relax over a glass of wine. However, if you're from a Latin country such as France, Italy or Spain, lunch is an occasion to connect and get to know the other person. The actual business can always come later, once trust has been established.

Another cultural difference – one which can create serious conflict if not handled properly – is the way disagreement is expressed. The Dutch, Germans and Israelis have no problem being blunt and direct in their criticism; it's not personal. If you're from England or the US, on the other hand, you would soften your criticism and couch it in more nuanced terms. And if you're from Japan, where people mustn't be seen to lose face, you would blur the message so that it can only be read between the lines.

It's easy to see how this culture-specific behaviour can lead to generalisations such as Germans are blunt, the British never say what they mean and the Japanese are inscrutable. National stereotypes can be both positive and negative. Successful, wealthy countries where people live in peace and prosperity attract admiration; dysfunctional countries plagued by poverty, crime and war do not. This is basic psychology: we admire winners, not losers. Of course, there are understandable reasons and mitigating circumstances for the plight of many struggling countries in Africa, South America and Asia. But stereotypes care little about this; they merely reflect the reality.

Russians, for example, don't enjoy a good image, and not just because of the war in Ukraine. It's simply that Russia is not regarded as a winning nation and evokes mostly negative associations.

Despite the end of communism more than thirty years ago, the country still lags behind the West both materially and socially[2], with a technologically backward economy unable to produce essential goods and services.[3] Crime, violence and alcoholism are big social problems. Russians speak English with a rough, harsh accent that comedians love to make fun of. They come across as grim and humourless – I had a Russian engineering lecturer at university who never smiled once in class during the entire year. In major holiday destinations, Russians have been described as rude and overbearing, and at one stage were ranked the worst tourists in the world, outdoing even the Germans.[4] This overall negative stereotype finds its ultimate expression in Hollywood movies, where Russians are generally portrayed as ruthless villains and cold-blooded killers.[5]

That said, losing nations can become winning nations and shake off their poor image.

Take China.

Back in the 1970s when I was in my teens, China was economically backward and desperately poor. Food was rationed, and much of the population was malnourished.[6] Most people rode bicycles and couldn't afford cars. They wore the same style of drab Mao suits (in deference to the Chinese leader, Chairman Mao); fashionable western clothing was seen as bourgeois and decadent. It was all about conformity. This is hardly the stuff of which positive stereotypes are made.

Today, some fifty years after bold economic reforms were instituted, China has become the second-largest economy behind the US, exporter to the world and a force to be reckoned with. The so-called Chinese growth miracle has lifted nearly a billion people out of poverty.[7] The country sends spacecraft to the moon, invests billions of dollars every year in Europe and the US, and is Africa's largest trading partner. The world's great department stores roll out the red carpet for wealthy Chinese tourists, hiring special staff just to cater to their needs.

Of course, that image has taken a hit in the economic aftermath of the Covid-19 pandemic. Nevertheless, the negative stereotype of decades ago is history. China has gone from being pitied to being admired – and perhaps even feared.

This shows how an enduring stereotype can change once the underlying reality that sustains it changes.

15

Ethnicity

A personal journey

I'M AN IDENTICAL TWIN. My twin brother and I grew up in Cape Town, South Africa, in the 1960s. Our parents were teachers, and we were solidly middle-class.

Under the government's system of racial classification – better known as apartheid – we were known as coloured, a term that denotes people of mixed race.[1] Their ancestry might go back one generation, several generations or even centuries. My great-grandfather on my father's side came from Scotland, while my grandfather on my mother's side came from India; both married coloured women. Tourists to South Africa are surprised to find that coloureds come in shades varying from white at one end to very brown at the other. They also learn that coloured is a generic term used in everyday discourse and in the media, unlike in the US, England and Australia, where it is politically loaded and best avoided.

Under apartheid, the main population groups – blacks, whites, coloureds and Indians – lived in separate neighbourhoods and led separate lives. We had very little social interaction with other races and hardly any direct experience of racial stereotyping.

When we were ten years old, our family left South Africa in search of greener pastures and settled in nearby Zambia, a former British colony. Only then did we start rubbing shoulders with people from other countries and cultures. How different they all looked and sounded!

The newly independent country was heavily reliant on foreign skills. At school and at university, our classmates were black, white, brown, olive-skinned and everything in between. Our teachers and lecturers came from Canada, the US, England, Scotland, Wales, Ireland, France, Denmark, Norway, Sweden, Finland, India, Pakistan, Bangladesh, Sri Lanka, Russia, South Africa and Mauritius – I may have left out a few. We soaked up all the different accents, facial features, clothing styles, cultural oddities and styles of teaching. Stereotyping was nothing unusual and came with the territory. To use a military metaphor, it was a target-rich environment.

Things became even more interesting after my brother and I fell in love with French at high school. It paved the way for a French-government scholarship to study aeronautical engineering in France. It was such an incredible adventure that I wrote a memoir about it, *The Scholarship Kids.*[2] That's when our stereotyping awareness really took off.

Walking around Nice airport during a brief stopover before continuing to Paris, we came across a French youth in shabby clothing at the entrance to the toilets. He held out his hand and asked for a few francs. A white person begging? That was a first for us. But we got an even greater shock inside when we saw that the women cleaning the toilets were also white! A lifetime of living in Africa had ingrained in us the notion that poverty and menial labour were associated with black people, not white people. Our preconceived notions were coming under severe pressure.

KEY TAKEAWAY: We all grow up with a specific ethnic view of the world that is strongly shaped by our environment and childhood experiences.

***

A couple of days later in Paris, we found ourselves in a taxi. The driver seemed fascinated by this pair of twins whose origins he couldn't quite place.

"Tell me something. I'm curious. You guys aren't black, but you aren't white either."

"Well, no ..."

"You're that colour – how does one say again? – *café au lait.*"

We found this hugely amusing. "*Café au lait*? That's very good! We must remember that."

The driver continued chatting as he weaved through the traffic. Occasionally, he would honk his horn and make exasperated gestures at other drivers.

"So where are you guys from?"

"South Africa."

"Yeah, but what country?"

"South Africa *is* a country."

"Never heard of it."

"C'mon, you're not serious! Johannesburg? Cape Town? Table Mountain?"

"Nope," he said, shaking his head.

My brother and I looked at each other in amused exasperation.

"Apartheid?"

"Huh?"

God, this was like pulling teeth. Suddenly, I had a brain-wave.

"The Springboks!"

"The rugby team?"

He was so excited that he turned to look at us, taking his eyes off the road for a moment. The franc had finally dropped.

"Yes, the rugby team."

"Well, whaddaya know!"

"So, you *have* heard of South Africa."

"No, but I have heard of the Springboks. I remember they played the French team once. They clobbered us." He laughed again, almost revelling in his own ignorance. "This is France, you know. Foreign countries don't really figure in the media here."

This surreal conversation repeated itself several times in the following months, not just with taxi drivers and shop-keepers, but also with university students and highly educated people who should have known better.

KEY TAKEAWAY: When you're in a foreign country, locals will naturally be curious about where you come from if it's not already clear from your looks or accent. Expect their knowledge of your country to be hazy and superficial.

***

After a few months in France, it soon became clear that we didn't fit into a neat stereotypical box. Being fluent in both French and English, we were hard to pin down. During a year-long internship at a French airline, we were occasionally taken for British and American. I have also been taken for someone from the French-speaking islands of Martinique, the

Seychelles, Mauritius and Madagascar, even though I have never set foot in any of these places.

In my experience, it's best to sail through such incidents with good humour. Even I have occasionally mistaken Canadians for Americans, Australians for New Zealanders, and Iranians for Arabs. I have also mispronounced foreign names more often than I care to remember, though probably not as often as others have mispronounced mine. "Gentle" is a particularly tough call for French-speakers, who tend to soften the "g" so that it sounds more like "Chantel".

Years later, after we had graduated, my brother was working at the Paris office of global telecoms company WorldCom. He travelled a lot and one day found himself in London with a team of French colleagues for a business meeting. Naturally, it was in English. Afterwards, his British host leaned over and whispered to him conspiratorially:

"You know, you speak really good English!"

"So do you!" my brother replied, not missing the opportunity for a snappy comeback.

They both had a good laugh. The man had obviously assumed him to be French.

KEY TAKEAWAY: People are doing the best they can with the information at their disposal (what you look and sound like), their knowledge of the world (mostly scanty) and their long-held biases and prejudices. It's unreasonable to expect them to always get it right, or to be offended if they don't.

***

Many years later, now working as a financial journalist for *Business Day* in Johannesburg, I got to visit the US for the first time. Within days of my arrival, I found myself in Washington DC on my way to interview a senior official at the Office of the Comptroller of the Currency, an independent bureau in the Treasury Department. I hailed a cab and hopped in. The driver was black. I could tell from his sing-song accent that he was from Nigeria. He was impressed that I knew this.

"Where are you from?"

"South Africa."

"Hey, I've got a friend in South Africa!"

We chatted easily. In the back seat sharing the ride with me was a middle-aged black woman. She listened with great interest. Then the conversation took a strange turn.

"You know why I picked you up?"

"Uh, because I needed a ride?"

"Because you're not black. You're obviously not from around here."

"You don't pick up black men?"

"Of course not. They do all the crime around here!"

His tone suggested this was self-evident. He then showed me the morning newspaper on the front passenger seat and pointed to an article about a taxi driver who'd been shot and killed the night before. It was front-page news.

"A black man did that, I tell you!"

I couldn't believe what I'd just heard. Far from taking offence, the black woman next to me nodded vigorously in agreement. It all sounded so normal, as if they were discussing the weather. I later related the incident to an official at the Office of the Comptroller of the Currency. He wasn't surprised. While cab drivers – irrespective of race – had no problem picking up black women and older black men, he explained, they avoided young black men for fear of being robbed.

I learned later during my month-long trip across the US that shopkeepers and security personnel often kept a close eye on black Americans in their stores, and that the police were more likely to stop them on the streets or pull them over in their cars.

Today, more than thirty years after that visit, a generally negative perception of African Americans as a group still has a firm hold on the national consciousness. Official statistics show they lag far behind other groups – particularly whites and Asians – in terms of earning power, education, home ownership, life expectancy and marriage rates.[3] Despite constituting barely 13% of the US population, black people are overrepresented[4] in violent crime such as robbery, murder and assault, and make up a significant proportion of the prison population[5]. Homicide is the leading cause of death among young black men.[6]

Police officers – both black and white – are more likely to shoot a black suspect believed to be armed than a white one. In various studies, this so-called shooter bias has even been measured in terms of the hesitation time before pulling the trigger.[7]

This overall negative stereotype gets a lot of media attention, which only anchors it further in people's minds. It invariably rubs off on ordinary black Americans, who often experience discrimination and negative stereotyping in their daily lives.[8] It might manifest, for example, in women clutching their handbags more tightly when a black man walks by, or drivers nervously locking their car doors.

KEY TAKEAWAY: The dominant reputation of your ethnic group – whether positive or negative, deserved or undeserved – will influence the way you are perceived and stereotyped.

***

Interestingly, once black Americans travel abroad for work, pleasure or to start a new life, the negative stereotype largely disappears. Whether in Spain, France or even Japan, they say that they are treated much better, feel a lot safer and aren't necessarily perceived as a threat. They're less conscious of being black and can just get on with their lives. Whatever racism they might encounter is simply not on the scale of what they knew back in America.

"It wasn't until I had left the USA to experience Spain that I really got a sense of what freedom looks like," a 28-year-old black woman from New York told *USA Today*, in an article on African Americans heading abroad to start a new life.[9]

This sudden change in perception of black Americans makes perfect sense. Back home, they are black; abroad, they're American. That's a huge stereotype shift right there. When they start a new life in a foreign country, it is not as marginalised members of society but as business owners, artists and highly skilled employees – and in Germany, as respected members of the US armed forces stationed there. The context is completely different.

A black American on the streets of Geneva or Berlin triggers a very different set of associations in the minds of the local populace – and the police – than in Chicago or New York. So, they react very differently, with no inherent distrust or suspicion.

KEY TAKEAWAY: Racial stereotyping isn't always about race. It also depends on the societal and cultural context, and how one is perceived in terms of social class, education and economic status.

16

Class

C LASS IS ONE OF those slippery, catch-all terms that is diffi-cult to define with any precision – but we know it when we see it.

To have class is to possess a powerful stereotype advantage in life. It leaves people favourably disposed towards you. One of the best things that can be said of a person once they have left the room is that they have class, or that they are a class act – and it is usually no act.

Dictionaries generally define class in terms of style, elegance and sophistication. This narrow definition fails to capture the complex, multifaceted and almost ineffable nature of the phe-nomenon. When a person has class, they possess a certain undefinable quality, a certain ...*je ne sais quoi.*

It's a subtle blend of build, looks, bearing, character, de-meanour, manners, etiquette, speech, values and emotional savvy.

Class is about standing up straight and carrying yourself properly; being quietly confident without being arrogant, and gracious without being fawning or obsequious. Class is about elegance and refinement, not ostentation or vulgarity. It's about good manners and etiquette. It's about speaking well rather than carelessly; listening more than talking; keeping calm rather than getting angry. Class is about respect, both for oneself and for others. Class values education yet wears its learning lightly. Class treads softly rather than heavily; whispers rather than shouts. Class is secure and has nothing to prove. It doesn't draw attention to itself or seek to make a statement; it is a statement in and of itself.

If you know your Bible, you will have noticed the eerie similarity with the definition of love in 1 Corinthians 13: 4-7 (English Standard Version): "Love is patient and kind; love does not envy or boast; it is not arrogant or rude. It does not insist on its own way; it is not irritable or resentful; it does not rejoice at wrongdoing, but rejoices with the truth. Love bears all things, believes all things, hopes all things, endures all things."

Are class and love simply different ways of expressing the universal ideal of a person at one with themselves, God and the world?

If the presence of class is hard to capture, its absence is not. We know someone has no class when they are cocky, arrogant or try too hard; when they are loud, dress ostentatiously or flaunt their wealth; when they don't take care of themselves and look a mess; when they are rude and condescending, especially to people of lower social status; when they speak poorly, swear or use slang; when they lack good manners and etiquette; when they mock learning and tout ignorance as a virtue; and when they have poor social skills. This virtually guarantees they will be negatively stereotyped – and treated accordingly. It's yet another illustration of a recurring theme throughout this book, namely that negative stereotypes generally emerge from characteristics perceived as negative or undesirable; the opposite is true for positive stereotypes.

Class is not synonymous with money, though money obviously helps. There are classy people who aren't wealthy or privileged; and there are wealthy, privileged people with no class. You only have to think of various public figures in business, politics and showbiz. Money can't buy you love, money can't buy you happiness and money certainly can't buy you class. Money comes and goes; class remains.

To be classy is to have internalised an attitude, a set of values and a way of seeing oneself and the world. It's doubtful whether it can be taught any more than maturity can be taught; both are something one probably grows into.

Yet it hasn't stopped people from trying. Class – often conflated with elegance – is one of the hottest topics in self-improvement and personal development. Coaches, business gurus and various experts sing its praises, portraying it as the silver bullet to getting ahead in life.

Internet searches on "How to be a class act", "How to be classy" or "The secrets of class" deliver countless articles, blog posts and videos. They cover everything from dress, manners and etiquette to confidence, values and language.

The tips on offer are surprisingly empowering. They put the responsibility for how people are perceived – in other words, their stereotype – on themselves rather than on others. Much emphasis is placed on taking responsibility for one's life instead of whining and complaining.

Of course, no one is going to instantly internalise these attributes and turn into a classy person overnight! But to be aware of them can be the first step on a much longer journey of personal growth.

17

Movies

T HE NEXT TIME YOU'RE watching a movie, notice how easy it is to tell the good guy from the bad guy in the opening scenes, even before they've said a single word. They just have a certain *look* about them.

We're all pretty good at reading movie characters. Within seconds, we know if they're, say, kind and helpful or mean and heartless.

That's because these characters are universal stereotypes. We recognise them instantly, even as infants. The same process is at work in real life when we encounter other people.

The influential Swiss psychologist Carl Jung called these generalisations archetypes.[1] They include the Father (a stern, powerful authority figure), the Hero (a champion, defender or rescuer) and the Trickster (a deceiver, liar or troublemaker). Jung reckoned these archetypes come from what he called the collective unconscious, a vast, cosmic memory bank of everything humanity has ever experienced.[2] They are innate, universal and hereditary. We are hardwired from birth to recognise them.

Other Jungian archetypes – he identified 12 – include the Ruler, the Sage, the Innocent, the Caregiver and the Rebel.

The notion of archetypes – or character types – is well anchored in literary fiction and draws on Jung's work.[3] For example, somebody who embodies the characteristics of a Leader (confident, brave, motivated) is well suited to the role of a president, CEO or captain of a sports team. At the other extreme, somebody who embodies the characteristics of a Caregiver (kind, generous, supportive) is well suited to the role of therapist, teacher or doctor.

Character types come in all shapes and sizes. In a classic teen movie set in a high school, you can't miss the nerd, the jock, the bully, the mean girl, the loner, the new kid, the misfit and the rebel. An entertaining online video titled *Top 10 Typical Movie Character Stereotypes* gives an excellent overview of the subject.[4]

Of course, good actors successfully play many different parts, but they are best suited to roles that correspond to their dominant character type. Actors are advised by their agents to stick to their character type to maximise their chances of landing a part.[5]

You're probably not going to see Tom Hanks playing an action hero any time soon, or Tom Cruise playing a Buddhist monk. Actors who play the same roles over and over are said to be typecast.[6] Examples are Dwayne Johnson (action movies), Hugh Grant in his prime (romantic comedies) and Melissa McCarthy (screwball comedies). Typecast actors may find that nobody will hire them to play any other role.

Whether we call these archetypes, stock characters or clichés, they're all ultimately a form of stereotype. They're a convenient mental shortcut. After all, you don't want viewers scratching their heads wondering what a certain character is doing in the story.

That's why casting a movie can take months.[7] Just as recruiters trawl through many résumés to decide who to bring in for a job interview, casting directors trawl through countless actor résumés to determine who to bring in for an audition. That number can run into hundreds when casting a new TV series – such as *Friends*, for example[8] – because it's so important to get the characters just right. Audiences have specific expectations of what a character should look and sound like. This is where smart stereotyping becomes critical.

If the story calls for a ruthless bank robber who shoots the security guard in the opening scene and beats a customer senseless, you're not going to cast a short, slightly built man with a high-pitched voice. It just jars stereotypically. Nobody would buy it.

Far better to cast a tall, rugged man with a deep, menacing voice and a craggy, pock-marked face that radiates evil. What about his social background? Probably someone of limited means who is sufficiently down on his luck to be driven to robbing a bank.

How about gender? Police statistics show that female bank robbers are rare. So, unless gender is relevant to the plot, you're probably better off sticking with a male character.

What about ethnicity? For an American mainstream movie, your safest bet would be somebody white. A black, Hispanic or Native-American villain in the lead role would be a tricky call, stereotypically speaking, unless it was pertinent to the story itself. Disadvantaged minority groups are generally represented either as victims or morally good people on the side of justice and decency.

An Asian-American or somebody Jewish as the bank robber would be just as tricky, stereotypically speaking. These are among the most successful ethnic groups in the US in terms of education, wealth and career success; there's no plausible motivation for them to be robbing banks.

If the bank robber was foreign, then casting him as Russian – perhaps from the Russian Mafia – would feel realistic. An upper-class Englishman? Perhaps, but then he would resort to wits and intelligence, not violence and thuggery. How about an Australian? The accent alone, with its comedic undertones, probably makes that a non-starter.

It's clear that stereotypes are a useful guide to casting a movie intelligently – or at least avoiding the most blatant mistakes.

In a romantic comedy, for example, you usually have a tall, handsome guy and an attractive girl. This is the norm across movie-making cultures, from Hollywood to Bollywood. You would not cast two short, overweight people with plain looks just to make a statement. Yes, these neglected outsiders fall in love, too, and their stories deserve to be told – but not in a mainstream romcom aimed at a mass audience.

Movies are first and foremost about entertainment. A long-running saying in Hollywood is if you want to send a message, use Western Union[9] – a reference to that company's original core business of transmitting and delivering telegram messages.

Going excessively against type or casting for reasons unrelated to the story – for example, to improve gender or racial representation – is a risky strategy and can result in a film that somehow feels off. It can also alienate fans and moviegoers.[10] Recent films that have come in for criticism for this reason are Amazon's *Lord of the Rings* series, and Disney's *The Little Mermaid* and *Snow White*.[11] Disney CEO Bob Iger, speaking at the 2023 DealBook Summit in New York, conceded the point when he said: "We have to entertain first. It's not about messages."[12]

Far from being undesirable, stereotypes are useful precisely because they anchor the movie in a reality the audience feels comfortable with.

18
Advertising

ADVERTISING HAS BEEN DESCRIBED as the art of arresting the intelligence long enough to get money from it.[1] Ads are short, so you'd better get your message across quickly and memorably. Easy-to-understand generalisations – or stereotypes – are an effective way of doing that.

This stereotype approach is the norm, whether it's in a black ad agency in Nairobi, a white ad agency in Stockholm or a Chinese ad agency in Beijing. There is no such thing as an advertisement that doesn't stereotype at some level.

This is easy to understand when you consider that an advertisement needs to target a certain demographic, which is just a fancy name for a specific segment of the population. Obvious demographic variables are age, gender, ethnicity, marital status, education, occupation and income. Others are home-ownership status, number of children, favourite brands, hobbies and interests, and perhaps even political affiliation.

The demographic for say, a Rolex or a Patek Philippe watch is very different from that for a Swatch or a Casio. The typical driver of a Porsche 911 is very different from the typical driver of a Kia Picanto.

All kinds of people fall into a given demographic – men, women; young, old; black, white and so forth. Ideally, you would design a tailor-made ad for each of them. Indeed, Japanese car manufacturer Subaru did just this in a famous campaign targeting five distinct groups that included medical professionals, rugged individualists and even lesbians.[2] However, this can be time-consuming and expensive. It's far more practical to design a one-size-fits-all ad around the average demographic profile.

This necessarily means stereotyping. You have to cast the "right" kind of people in terms of age, looks, ethnicity, gender, education and social standing.[3] They shouldn't stray too far from the societal expectations of your consumers.

Take the advertising of household products.

Despite greater gender equality in recent decades, women still do the lion's share of traditional household chores such as cleaning, washing and cooking – not to mention taking care of the kids.[4] Men may occasionally stack the dishwasher or run the vacuum cleaner, but they're more likely to be mowing the lawn, cleaning the car or fixing things. Household chores are gender-specific, and so is the responsibility for who buys what. The woman is more likely to choose the vacuum cleaner, whereas the man is more likely to choose the DIY toolset.

So, if you're selling detergents, dishwashing liquid or washing machines, it makes sense to pitch your ads at women. If you're selling lawnmowers, ladders or handheld drills, it makes sense to pitch your ads at men. That's just the commercial reality. Casting characters who clash with your customers' expectations or fall too far outside their societal frame of reference, stereotypically speaking, is a risky strategy. It can alienate your key demographic, compromise brand loyalty and hit sales.

A case in point was American brewing company Anheuser-Busch's decision in 2023 to use a transgender woman to promote Bud Light, its hugely popular beer brand. It provoked a consumer backlash, unleashed a storm of negative media commentary and sent sales plummeting by around 20% within a month.[5] The divisive ad campaign was quietly dropped and replaced with something more traditional.

Gillette, maker of razors and personal-care products, ran into a similar problem in 2019 with a campaign that waded into the #*MeToo* controversy, with its accusations of toxic masculinity. It was praised by some observers, but it also unleashed a flood of negative commentary online, led to calls for a boycott and quickly became one of the most disliked videos on YouTube.[6] A common objection was that men buy razors to shave, not to be lectured to about their behaviour.

Of course, there are many creative ads that seek to break traditional gender stereotypes, and the annual Cannes Glass Lion award recognises the best of them.[7] What is less clear, however, is whether such advertisements are truly effective in terms of sales.

In any event, you may have replaced a man with a woman in your ad for handheld drills, but you're still stereotyping in terms of her looks and social class. You may have replaced the skinny, attractive blonde in the clothing ad with a plain-looking, full-figured brunette, but she's still a stereotype in terms of what customers find acceptable. So, we're not so much shattering stereotypes as playing around with them at the margins. Even when you don't want to stereotype, you still have to stereotype – it just happens at another level.

Take personal-care company Dove's 2004 Campaign for Real Beauty, which successfully took a stand against unrealistic beauty standards by featuring a bevy of naturally curvy women.[8] It's obvious from the stunning pictures that the women were carefully curated to fall within acceptable beauty standards. These were not random choices: lovely faces, gorgeous smiles, smooth skin and not a trace of cellulite in sight.

There's not a single fat, unattractive, pimple-plagued "real" woman among them.

Like it or not, we still want our ads inhabited by glamourous, attractive, successful people whose lifestyle we envy and aspire to. Nobody wants to buy products promoted by physically unattractive people, or those perceived to be a failure in life; that's just basic psychology. For better or for worse, our consumer impulses are shaped by positive stereotypes.

19
Cars

D O WE STEREOTYPE CARS and the people who drive them? Absolutely.

When I see a BMW in my rear-view mirror, I tense and grip the steering wheel more tightly. That's because I know what's probably coming next. He (most BMW drivers are men) is going to flash his headlights and race up my tail to get me to go faster. If that fails, he'll overtake aggressively and cut back dangerously in front of me before roaring off into the distance.

This happens often enough to be a statistical probability. In other words, it's a stereotype. I find that it's most common with the smaller models such as the 3-Series rather than the larger, luxury 7-Series. On rare occasions, I'll see a BMW hanging back patiently at a safe following distance. It reminds me not to leap to judgement too hastily.

Of course, such stereotyping cuts both ways: I can easily imagine the BMW driver thinking, *Oh, no – not another old fart in a Honda!*

BMW drivers are generally pushy and aggressive. This has been confirmed in different studies done on both sides of the Atlantic, according to *The Wall Street Journal*.[1] For example, they are the least likely to stop at a pedestrian crossing and the most likely to try to push through at a four-way intersection.

The car we drive is a projection of our inner selves.[2] It tells people about our values and how we see the world – think electric Tesla versus gas-guzzling Range Rover. It speaks volumes about our income, behaviour and social class. Who are you more likely to want to rent your home to – the applicant who pulls up sedately in the driveway in a grey Volvo sedan, or the one who squeals to a halt in a red Chevrolet Corvette? If a man picks you up for a date in his white Toyota Camry, what is he more likely to be: reckless and exciting, or dependable and reliable?

We treat cars on the road just like we treat people – with courtesy, rudeness or indifference. Some cars we like, others we don't. And it's not just about the make and model; we're even influenced by how clean a car is.

Once during a visit to New York, I took a short driving holiday to nearby Newport, Rhode Island, famous for its historic mansions and rich sailing history. Keen to experience an American automotive icon, I splashed out on a beautiful, burgundy-coloured Cadillac rental car. I was positively stereotyped wherever I went. Policemen fell over themselves to be helpful whenever I stopped to ask for directions; motorists courteously let me through at intersections; and onlookers would nod friendly greetings and eye the car admiringly. There was a clear halo effect going on!

This was no random occurrence. In more than thirty years of owning and renting different cars, from small urban runarounds to larger luxury sedans, I've detected a definite pattern: the larger and more expensive my car, the more courteously I am treated on the roads. Of course, my generally relaxed driving style is also a factor, but by no means the only one.

Car stereotypes are a humorous topic of discussion among motoring journalists, car aficionados and bloggers.[3] For example, powerful muscle cars and obscenely huge pick-up trucks are driven by rugged, macho men. Sedate luxury sedans are driven by boring, elderly men. Cute, small cars with bright colours are driven by trendy young women. And what do moms drive to ferry the kids around? Practical SUVs or minivans known as MPVs (multi-purpose vehicles – or, perhaps more accurately, mommy-purpose vehicles).

These stereotypes are surprisingly reliable. Try switching them around and see how absurd they become. For example, muscle cars and obscenely huge pick-up trucks are driven by trendy young women, while small, brightly coloured cars are driven by rugged, macho men.

A case in point is the hugely successful Fiat 500, with its bubble shape and retro 1960s styling. It is an absolute hit with female drivers, who have voted it the sexiest car on the road. It has been described as a brightly coloured Easter Egg and a handbag on wheels. Male motoring journalists who have tried it out report receiving strange stares from bemused onlookers and other drivers.[4] Another car with a huge female following is the Mini Cooper. Women say they love the bright colours, the stylish retro design, and its compactness and manoeuvrability.

When it comes to splashing out on a new set of wheels, men and women have very different preferences.[5] Even in an age of SUVs, men still like large, low-slung cars with wide tyres and muscular curves, while women prefer smaller, more compact cars with cleaner lines. Men look for size and power; women look for safety, practicality and a cute design. A man describing his new car would proudly boast about its 3.5-litre, V6 turbo engine, while a woman would delight in the cherry-red exterior and cream upholstery.

Do cars project a certain look and personality by virtue of their headlights (the eyes), the grille or emblem (the nose) and the air-intake (the mouth)? When we see a car, do we also see a face?

Apparently, we do, according to an American study.[6] Participants were shown reconstructions and images of nearly forty different brands of car. Fully one-third of them associated a human face or animal face with at least 90% of the cars. And nearly all of them agreed on whether a car looked dominant or submissive. British research has shown that certain cars are consistently rated as more aggressive than others, depending on the make, model and colour.[7] Out on the road, the age and gender of the driver also plays a role, with a young man at the wheel being perceived as more aggressive than an older man or a woman.

So, clearly, a car is not just a hunk of metal that leaves people indifferent as it goes by. It triggers associations, both positive and negative, that play out as enduring stereotypes.

20

Artificial intelligence (AI)

G RACE, SOPHIA, ERICA, HARMONY, Jia Jia: these are some of the world's most prominent robots. And yes, they're all female.[1]

They have pleasing names that roll easily off the tongue. They are all white, or at least very fair. They speak well, often with a posh accent. They're classically cute or pretty – Jia Jia, from China, is said to be the most beautiful woman in the land. They have straight hair, well-proportioned faces, soft features and round eyes.

Can you spot the common denominator? Yes, these are all favourable stereotypes. They make the robots likeable and non-threatening, so people are more likely to want to interact with them. Studies show that female robots are perceived as more human than male robots, with more positive human qualities. They are seen as warmer, and more likely to experience emotions.[2]

This kind of technology-stereotyping is nothing new.

Take the GPS navigation system in your car, which invariably has a female voice. The same goes for the well-known voice assistants Alexa (Amazon) and Siri (Apple).[3] An assistant is supposed to be helpful and supportive, and a female voice embodies these characteristics better than a male voice. In tests, both male and female subjects systematically prefer a female voice.[4] In certain languages like French and Arabic, however, Siri may default to a male voice.[5] In Germany, BMW recalled a GPS system from one of its car models after many German men said they didn't want to take instructions from a woman![6]

The current preponderance of white, female AI technology has led to concerns about racism and sexism.[7] Female voice assistants, in particular, are said to entrench the stereotypical image of women as carers and helpers, both at home and in the workplace.

"Why aren't there more black robots?" some ask, amid calls for more diversity. It was even the subject of a study by the University of Canterbury in New Zealand. It found that people hold the same automatic biases towards darker-coloured robots as they do towards darker-coloured people.[8]

Then again, AI is a business like any other. Its products and services are designed to appeal to different customer segments. These include children, hotel guests, restaurant patrons, hospital patients and elderly people living alone or in retirement villages. Manufacturers are simply responding to their expectations and preferences around what a robot should look and sound like. If there turns out to be a market for male robots of a darker hue – and why shouldn't there be? – you can be sure that manufacturers will cash in and fill the gap.

Indeed, there are times when the authority associated with a male voice might actually be a good thing – for example, in an emergency requiring the immediate evacuation of a burning building or a ship in distress. Similarly, the strength and physicality associated with men is something manufacturers might conceivably exploit when designing a robot for a harsh environment – for example, a construction site or the battlefield.

The market for robots is still in its infancy. As it evolves to meet widely different needs and customer segments – as was the case after the invention of the automobile, for example – a wider range of styles and colours will inevitably emerge.

Artificial intelligence has also been accused of bias. The official term is algorithmic bias, defined as systematic and repeatable errors that create unfair outcomes, such as favouring one group over another.[9]

Way back in the early 1980s, dozens of candidates were denied entry to St George's Hospital Medical School in London because the algorithm designed to help with the assessments had been instructed to exclude applicants with foreign-sounding names.[10] In 2015, Amazon's recruitment algorithm developed to screen job applications was found to be inadvertently excluding female applicants because of the way it was interpreting the résumés.[11] Such cases lend credence to the quip, often attributed to Albert Einstein, that artificial intelligence is no match for natural stupidity.[12]

It's true that AI is biased, but not in the traditional sense of the word.

At the risk of trivialising a stupendous feat of technological inventiveness, AI is nothing more than a pile of components, wires and computer chips. It has no consciousness. It cannot grasp notions of morality, fairness or even reality itself. It can tell a cat from a dog, but it doesn't really know what either is. All it can do is analyse the data it is given, detect patterns and draw conclusions. For example, AI can detect breast cancer by examining X-rays; it can guide a self-driving car by reading the surrounding environment; and it can crunch vast volumes of research findings and identify interesting conclusions for policymakers.

So-called generative AI, which burst onto the scene recently in the form of ChatGPT and similar tools, can even generate content such as text, imagery and audio.[13] However, it can only do this from the information it is trained on. It can't think from scratch.

In an interesting experiment to test AI's ability to produce original thought, an eminent French philosopher went up against ChatGPT to answer the question "Is happiness a matter of reason?", taken from a high-school examination paper. The scoring panel gave him a perfect 100%, while ChatGPT scraped through with 55%, despite having been extensively trained and prepped. Apparently, the AI answer – produced in just over ten minutes – was little more than a succession of impressive-sounding phrases, without any real reflection or sustained argument.[14]

AI bias is particularly apparent in the generation of images. An artificially generated picture of, say, a CEO or scientist, is far more likely to show a man rather than a woman, and one who is white rather than black. That's because, in western countries at any rate, these professions are indeed largely white and male. The algorithm is merely making rational inferences from the data; in other words, it stereotypes. For the same reason, an artificially generated image of a professional American basketball player is likely to show a black man, because black men make up just over 70% of the players in the National Basketball Association.[15] For better or for worse, AI crunches the data of the world as it is, with all its skewed representation, and not as some might like it to be.

Trying to adjust images for diversity can have unintended consequences, as Google discovered in February 2024 with its new AI tool, Gemini. The company was forced to take Gemini's image generator offline after women and people of colour showed up in images of Nazi soldiers, the Pope and even the American Founding Fathers.[16] These false depictions unleashed a flood of negative reaction,[17] with certain critics accusing Google of trying to rewrite history and force a diversity agenda on the world.[18]

Clearly, bias is as normal in artificial intelligence as it is in human beings, and neither could function without it. Of course, algorithms could be improved, but that's more about smarter programming and better training data.

A computer scientist from the University of Southern California argues that attempts to mitigate AI bias or avoid sensitive topics can actually make things worse by producing misleading or incomplete content. He reckons AI should be allowed to be biased, with users being able to specify the levels of bias they want to work with.[19]

This is already happening. The increasing number of ChatGPT lookalikes coming onto the market all have different political biases, ranging from very left-wing to very right-wing. This naturally affects how they answer questions and generate content.[20]

That's not necessarily a bad thing. It means that differently biased AI systems can compete in the marketplace and appeal to different consumer segments. This is exactly how the media landscape works, where we choose our newspapers, radio stations and television channels depending on their editorial bias.

And you can be sure that billionaire entrepreneur Elon Musk's much-vaunted Grok chatbot, described in the press as anti-woke,[21] will be somewhere in the mix.

21

Humour

PERHAPS NOTHING ILLUSTRATES THE universality of stereo-typing more than humour. All over the world, people poke fun at each other's differences, shortcomings and idiosyncrasies. It seems as if everyone is fair game for a joke, witticism or put-down:

- Police are looking for a gang of gay men who break into homes in the middle of the night and rearrange the furniture.

- What goes clippety-clop, clippety-clop – BANG! BANG! – clippety-clop, clippety-clop? An Amish drive-by shooting.

- Why was the bee flying around New York with a yarmulke on his head? He didn't want to be mistaken for a WASP.

- An American tourist visiting historic Windsor Castle looks upwards as a plane passes overhead on its way to land at Heathrow. He turns to his wife: "This castle is really cool, but why did they have to build it so close to the airport?"

- What do you call an Italian with only one arm? Someone with a speech impediment.

If you found any of these funny or at least understood them, then you were in on the joke. Humour relies on a shared understanding. If you tell me a joke underpinned by a stereotype, I need to be aware of it – or at least find it plausible.

When I first started working in France, the subject of a colleague's work habits came up in conversation. He did his work well, but no more and no less.

"Oh, what do you expect?" said a team-member, "He's from Corsica!"

They both laughed, including the Corsican. I didn't get it.

"Have you never heard the expression 'as lazy as a Corsican'?!"

It turned out that people from the French island of Corsica in the Mediterranean supposedly have a reputation for being lazy. I was blissfully unaware of this, so the remark flew right over my head. Eventually, the various French ethnic and inter-cultural jokes started to make sense. Here's one I was told about marginalised youths from the Arab community:

Mohammed and Abdul are seated in the back of a car. Who's driving? The police.

But it's the Belgians who get the short end of the stick in France. There is a massive compendium of jokes, one-liners and vignettes – known as *les histoires belges* – all based on the premise that people from Belgium aren't very bright. I've heard them being told in the playground, in the office, and on radio and television. Much like blonde jokes, it's all very good-natured and jocular. The Belgians shrug it off and seem to take it in their stride.

That's probably because they're too busy making fun of the Dutch, whom they see as stingy and tight-fisted ("How does a Dutch dessert recipe begin? Borrow 200 g of butter, 50 g of sugar and a litre of milk..."). Indeed, the whole of western Europe is like a comedy club in which the different nationalities constantly make fun of each other. The humble Portuguese mock the haughty Spanish; the sophisticated British mock the rural Irish; and struggling Poles make fun of overbearing, successful Germans. What about the Swiss? They don't do humour ("How do you make someone from Switzerland laugh? You hold a gun to their head and say: laugh, dammit!").

This form of humour is a great European tradition, according to Romain Seignovert, author of *De qui se moque-t-on?* (*Who Are We Making Fun of?*), a book on the jokes Europeans tell about their neighbours. "We are a big, diverse community with a centuries-long common history of highs and lows, and our humour reflects that," he says in an article in *The Guardian*.[1]

But if you really want to get to grips with stereotype humour, you can do no better than dive into the successful works of Bulgarian-born writer and cartographer Yanko Tsvetkov. His full-colour *Atlas of Prejudice* shows maps in which countries are represented not by their names, but by their stereotypes. It is riotously funny. [2]

It's difficult these days to find jokes that openly make fun of other people. When idly browsing in major bookstores, whether in Johannesburg, Lisbon or Paris, I struggle to find such material on open display. Have we all become wimps, so lacking in self-worth that we can't handle the cut-and-thrust of everyday humour? Back when I was at university, joke books were required reading. They sat openly on our bookshelves, along with our textbooks. They ran the gamut from black jokes,

Jewish jokes and Polish jokes to blonde jokes, dementia jokes and even leprosy jokes ("How did the leper end the poker game? He threw his hand in."). If this makes you squirm, then you're probably of a more recent generation that grew up with a very different set of social norms and also probably never read the satirical *Mad* magazine.[3]

One of the most-borrowed books in our university library was *Rationale of the Dirty Joke: An Analysis of Sexual Humor*, by American cultural critic Gershon Legman. This hefty tome analyses more than two thousand jokes and folktales from a social, psychological and historical perspective. It's still available on Amazon, but with a sticker on the front cover that reads PARENTAL ADVISORY – EXPLICIT CONTENT.[4] Seriously?! Children probably don't even know what *rationale* means.

It's a sad indictment of our times that people need to be sheltered in this way. Humour is integral to being human, and something that people of all ages and cultures respond to. Even in the depths of despair in German concentration camps during World War II, Jewish prisoners told each other jokes to keep their spirits up. A sense of humour is a vital social skill, and it's well established scientifically that laughter contributes to both physical and psychological well-being.

Of course, there's a time and place for humour. The joke you tell at the dinner table or with your friends over a beer won't necessarily go down well during a client meeting or a presentation to shareholders. And what got a surefire laugh twenty years ago might be greeted by a stony silence today, because times change. But it's precisely exposure to all kinds of humour in an accepting and tolerant environment that allows us to recognise this. Walking the fine line between outrage and laughter is not learned by avoiding jokes for fear of giving offence.

As American writer Max Eastman observed, it's the ability to take a joke, not make one, that proves you have a sense of humour.[5]

Conclusion

A TTRACTIVE, PLAIN, TALL, SHORT, male, female, gay, young, old, black, white, brown, blonde, brunette, straight hair, curly hair, kind, generous, smiling, scowling, formally dressed, casually attired, well-spoken, intelligent, high-status, low-status, BMW-driving, Chanel-wearing, American, French, Australian, classy, rude, polite, well-behaved, liberal, conservative, Muslim, Christian...

The number of ways in which we all differ from one another is mind-numbingly long – certainly much more than just twenty-one. Throw in all the distinct characteristics associated with each of them, and the permutations become endless. Is it any wonder that we stereotype?

It's the brain's way of reducing complexity and facilitating decision-making, and it does this without needing our conscious approval. We are effectively on autopilot in every waking moment, systematically processing and categorising the people we encounter in the world, noting their similarities and distinct characteristics.

These categories are stored in memory as convenient stereotypes. They enable us to draw tentative conclusions about a person without knowing everything about them. These conclusions can be positive, neutral or negative. It's a mental shortcut. Without it, we would be forced to repeatedly evaluate people anew, as if for the very first time, with no useful frame of reference or basis of comparison. This is a recipe for cognitive overload and would lead to paralysis through analysis.

Contrary to the dominant narrative on the subject, stereotyping is not something we should stop doing – that is neurologically impossible. And even if we were brave enough to try, the sheer number of distinct stereotype categories means we would have to police our thoughts and second-guess ourselves to the point of mental exhaustion. Stereotyping is not a shortcoming of human nature either that somehow needs to be fixed or outsmarted – it fulfils its primary task of reducing complexity and facilitating decision-making. It's not perfect, but then no aspect of the human condition ever is. Neither is stereotyping some sort of evolutionary baggage left over from our caveman days when it was vital for quickly recognising threats from predators and foes; it remains an integral part of our cognitive apparatus – and all the more so in today's complex and multifaceted world.

In short, stereotyping isn't a problem to be solved; rather, it is a reality to be understood. Only then can we learn how to live with it instead of trying to wish it out of existence.

As the countless scenarios, studies and anecdotes throughout the book have shown – and probably your own personal experience, too – there is a logic to stereotyping that goes beyond mere sexism, racism, ageism or any other "ism". Of course, it is naïve to think these do not exist, but it is just as naïve to systematically attribute all stereotyping to them, for these are hardly the default settings of most people. For example, in answering the questions to the quiz at the beginning of the book, did you think of yourself in these accusatory terms? If anything, you probably saw yourself as making fairly rational choices, and for reasons that were rather obvious.

When all is said and done, it's hard to escape the conclusion that stereotyping is mostly common sense. And for all its imperfections, it is far more reliable than we give it credit for. It constantly provides us with useful and predictive information that helps us get through the day. It conveniently oils the wheels of our social interactions, helping us to evaluate each other while also keeping us safe.

Sure, stereotyping is sometimes hurtful, but so is criticism, blame, rejection, loss, heartbreak and the countless slings and arrows of human existence. Stereotyping seems almost trivial by comparison. It's nothing that a mature adult with a half-decent sense of self cannot handle, and perhaps even shrug off.

Stereotyping is something to embrace with pragmatism and good sense. It is an equal-opportunity cognitive function that we all get to benefit from and that leaves us all better off.

About the author

Robert Gentle is a former engineer and journalist. He has lived and worked in South Africa, Zambia, France, England and the United States. E-mail: *rgentle@icon.co.za*

Acknowledgements

Special thanks to my twin brother Michael for his sterling work in improving successive drafts of the manuscript. To my niece Marina and my nephew Kevin: *merci pour le feedback!* And finally, a shout-out to editorial consultant Russel Brownlee for his insightful analysis of the initial draft.

Bibliography

1. BOOTH, Michael
   The Almost Nearly Perfect People: Behind the Myth of the Scandinavian Utopia (London: Vintage, 2015)

2. COBB, Jelani; REMNICK David
   The Matter of Black Lives: Writing from The New Yorker (Glasgow, UK: William Collins, 2021)

3. ETCOFF, Nancy
   Survival of the Prettiest: The Science of Beauty (New York: Anchor Books, 2000)

4. GENTLE, Robert
   The Scholarship Kids (Cape Town: Melinda Ferguson Books, 2023)

5. GOLDMAN, William
   Adventures in the Screen Trade: A Personal View of Hollywood (New York: Warner Books, 1984)

6. GRAY, John
   Men Are From Mars, Women Are From Venus (New York: HarperCollins, 1992)

7. GUILIANO, Mireille
   French Women Don't Get Fat: The Secret of Eating for Pleasure (New York: Vintage Books, 2007)

8. JUSSIM, Lee
   Social Perception and Social Reality: Why Accuracy Dominates Bias and Self-Fulfilling Prophecy (Oxford, UK: Oxford University Press, 2012)

9. KAHNEMAN, Daniel
   Thinking, Fast and Slow (London: Penguin, 2012)

10. LEGMAN, Gershon
    Rationale of the Dirty Joke: An Analysis of Sexual Humor (New York: Grove Press, 1968)

11. MATHER, Victoria
    Absolutely Typical: The Best of Social Stereotypes from the Telegraph Magazine (North Yorkshire: Methuen, 1996)

12. McGARTY, Craig; YZERBYT, Vincent Y; SPEARS, Russel
    Stereotypes as Explanations: The Formation of Meaningful Beliefs about Social Groups (Cambridge, UK: Cambridge University Press, 2002)

13. MEYER, Erin
    The Culture Map: Decoding How People Think, Lead, and Get Things Done Across Cultures (New York: Public Affairs, 2015)

14. MORAN, Caitlin
    What About Men? A Feminist Answers the Question (London: Ebury Press, 2023)

15. OGILVY, David
Ogilvy on Advertising (New York: Vintage Books, 1985)

16. PEASE, Allan; PEASE, Barbara
Why Men Don't Listen and Women Can't Read Maps
(New York, Broadway Books, 2001)

17. SASTRE, Peggy
La domination masculine n'existe pas (Paris: Anne
Carrière, 2015)

18. SCHNEIDER, David J
The Psychology of Stereotyping (New York, The Guild-
ford Press, 2005).

19. SEIGNOVERT, Romain
De qui se moque-t-on? Tour d'Europe en 345 blagues
(Paris: Opportun, 2016)

20. SOWELL, Thomas
Race and Culture: A World View (New York: Basic
Books, 1995)

21. TROMPENAARS,   Fons;   HAMPDEN-TURNER
Charles
*Riding the Waves of Culture: Understanding Diversity
in Global Business* (New York: McGraw Hill, 2012)

22. TSVETKOV, Yanko
*Atlas of Prejudice: The Complete Stereotype Map Col-
lection* (Alphadesigner, 2016)

References

The man on the platform
1. Randolph M Nesse, "The smoke detector principle: Signal detection and optimal defense regulation", *Evolution Medicine and Public Health* (Volume 2019, Issue 1, 2019, Page 1), https://doi.org/10.1093/emph/eoy034

2. "Bounded rationality", Wikipedia, (23 April, 2024), https://en.wikipedia.org/wiki/Bounded_rationality

3. Noam Shpancer, "Stereotype Accuracy: A Displeasing Truth", *Psychology Today* (September 20, 2018), https://www.psychologytoday.com/za/blog/insight-therapy/201809/stereotype-accuracy-displeasing-truth

4. Lee Jussim, "Truth in stereotypes", *Aeon* (15 August, 2016), https://aeon.co/essays/truth-lies-and-stereotypes-when-scientists-ignore-evidence

5. Ellie Mulcahy, "When and how do children learn prej-

udice?",
The Centre for Education & Youth (12 December, 2017),
https://cfey.org/2017/12/children-learn-prejudice/

6. "Simplifying our world",
Max-Planck-Gesellschaft (April 21, 2021),
https://www.mpg.de/16747094/0416-psy-simplifying
-our-world-155111-x

CHAPTER 1: Attractiveness
1. "Beauty",
Wikipedia (24 April, 2024),
https://en.wikipedia.org/wiki/Beauty#As_an_
attribute_to_humans

2. Alan Slater, Charlotte Von der Schulenburg, Elizabeth
Brown, Marion Badenoch, George Butterworth, Sonia
Parsons, Curtis Samuels, "Newborn infants prefer attractive faces,"
Infant Behavior and Development (Volume 21, Issue 2,
1998), Pages 345-354, ISSN 0163-6383,
https://doi.org/10.1016/S0163-6383(98)90011-X,
(https://www.sciencedirect.com/science/article/pii/S0
16363839890011X)

3. "Golden Ratio Face: Facial Beauty & Proportions",
Centre for Surgery,
https://centreforsurgery.com/facial-beauty-stan-
dards-golden-ratio/

4. "Physical attractiveness",
Wikipedia (24 April, 2024),
https://en.wikipedia.org/wiki/Physical_attractive-

ness#General_contributing_factors

5. Ibid.

6. Ibid.

7. Ibid.

8. Allana Akhtar and Drake Baer, "11 scientific reasons why attractive people are more successful in life", *Business Insider* (updated October 8, 2019), https://www.businessinsider.com/beautiful-people-make-more-money-2014-11

9. Daniel S. Hamermesh, "Beauty Pays: Why Attractive People Are More Successful", *(Princeton University Press, 2013)*, https://press.princeton.edu/books/paperback/9780691158174/beauty-pays

10. Chelsea Fagan, "We Need To Talk About Pretty Privilege", *The Financial Diet* (July 25, 2023), https://www.youtube.com/watch?v=VI3mwVhoh1A

11. Tomas Chamorro-Premuzic, "It's Time To Expose The Attractiveness Bias At Work", *Forbes* (July 17, 2019), https://www.forbes.com/sites/tomaspremuzic/2019/07/17/its-time-to-expose-the-attractiveness-bias-at-work/

12. Michael Woudenberg, "The Beauty Quandary", *Polymathic Being* (September 17, 2023), https://www.polymathicbeing.com/p/the-beau-

ty-quandary

13. Beaver KM, Boccio C, Smith S, Ferguson CJ. "Physical attractiveness and criminal justice processing: results from a longitudinal sample of youth and young adults." *Psychiatr Psychol Law*. 2019 Jul 8;26(4):669-681. doi: 10.1080/13218719.2019.1618750. PMID: 31984103; PM-CID: PMC6762156. https://www.ncbi.nlm.nih.gov/pmc/articles/PMC6762156/

14. Matt Parrett, "Beauty and the feast: Examining the effect of beauty on earnings using restaurant tipping data", *Journal of Economic Psychology*, (Volume 49, 2015), Pages 34-46, ISSN 0167-4870, https://doi.org/10.1016/j.joep.2015.04.002, (https://www.sciencedirect.com/article/pii/S01674870 1500046X)

15. Jack Schafer, "Six Tips to Get Higher Tips", *Psychology Today* (July 18, 2012), https://www.psychologyto-day.com/za/blog/let-their-words-do-the-talk-ing/201207/six-tips-to-get-higher-tips

16. Elizabeth Hoyt, "Attractive Students Get Higher Grades, According to Study", *Fastweb* (April 4, 2018), https://www.fastweb.com/student-life/arti-cles/more-attractive-students-get-higher-grades-ac-cording-to-study

17. "Study Explores Why Attractive Students Get Better

Grades",
WIA Report (November 23, 2022),
https://www.wiareport.com/2022/11/study-explores-why-attractive-students-get-better-grades/

18. Pepper Schwartz, "When teachers favor attractive kids",
CNN (January 2, 2014),
https://edition.cnn.com/2014/01/02/opinion/schwartz-attractiveness-teens/index.html

19. Rodrigo Praino, "How a candidate's looks may be swinging your vote (without you even realising it)",
The Conversation (December 2, 2018),
https://theconversation.com/how-a-candidates-looks-may-be-swinging-your-vote-without-you-even-realising-it-107364

20. Stockemer, D., Praino, R., "The Good, the Bad and the Ugly: Do Attractive Politicians Get a 'Break' When They are Involved in Scandals?",
Polit Behav **41**, 747-767 (2019),
https://doi.org/10.1007/s11109-018-9469-1

21. "Halo effect,"
Wikipedia (24 April, 2024),
https://en.wikipedia.org/wiki/Halo_effect

22. "Horn effect,"
Wikipedia (24 April, 2024),
https://en.wikipedia.org/wiki/Horn_effect

23. "Lookism",
Wikipedia (24 April, 2024),

https://en.wikipedia.org/wiki/Lookism

24. "Nancy Etcoff",
Wikipedia (2 May, 2024),
https://en.wikipedia.org/wiki/Nancy_Etcoff#Personal_life

25. "The Beauty Myth",
Wikipedia (30 May, 2024),
https://en.wikipedia.org/wiki/The_Beauty_Myth

CHAPTER 2: Height
1. Gert Stulp, Abraham P. Buunk, Thomas V. Pollet, "Women want taller men more than men want shorter women", *Personality and Individual Differences*, (Volume 54, Issue 8), 2013, Pages 877-883, ISSN0191-8869, https://doi.org/10.1016/j.paid.2012.12.019, (https://www.sciencedirect.com/science/article/pii/S0191886913000020)

2. Jonathan Owen, "Tall people more likely to be successful in life, study finds",
The Independent (9 March,2016),
https://www.independent.co.uk/life-style/health-and-families/health-news/tall-people-more-likely-to-be-successful-in-life-study-find-a6919431.html

3. LEX Opinion, "CEO height: the long and short of it", *Financial Times*, (August 6, 2023), https://www.ft.com/content/bb548d31-aa6b-4700-8c0c-3cc623b7376f

4. Gert Stulp, Abraham P. Buunk, SimonVerhulst, Thomas V. Pollet, "Tall claims? Sense and nonsense about the

importance of height of US presidents", *The Leadership Quarterly*,(Volume 24, Issue 1) 2013, Pages 159-171, ISSN 1048-9843,https://doi.org/10.1016/j.leaqua.2012.09.002. https://www.sciencedirect.com/science/article/pii/S1048984312000884)

5. "Heights of presidents and presidential candidates of the United States",
Wikipedia (19 May, 2024),
https://en.wikipedia.org/wiki/Heights_of_presidents_
and_presidential_candidates_of_the_United_States
#Comparative_table_of_heights_of_United_States_
presidential_candidates

6. Emine Saner, "Famous men who need a little lift",
The Guardian (9 April, 2009),
https://www.theguardian.com/lifeandstyle/2009/
apr/09/shortcuts-celebrity-stack-heels

7. "CelebHeights",
https://www.celebheights.com/

8. Reviewed by Sheri Jacobson, "Small Man Syndrome",
Harley Therapy (January 29, 2019),
https://harleytherapy.com/blog/posts/
small-man-syndrome

9. Knapen JEP, Blaker NM, Van Vugt M. "The Napoleon Complex: When Shorter Men Take More.",
Psychol Sci. 2018 Jul;29(7):1134-1144. doi: 10.1177/0956797618772822. Epub 2018 May 10. PMID: 29746217; PMCID: PMC6247438.
https://www.ncbi.nlm.nih.gov/pmc/articles/PMC6247438/

10. Joseph P. Tucker, "Average Bodybuilders' Height: See How Tall Most Are In cm", *Max Health Living* (January 10, 2024), https://maxhealthliving.com/how-tall-are-most-body builders/

11. Daniel Louwrens, "Average Bodybuilder Height and Sizes: Statistics, and Facts", *Muscle and Brawn* (updated April 3, 2023), https://muscleandbrawn.com/statistics/ bodybuilder-height/

12. M. Dittmann, "Standing tall pays off, study finds", American Psychological Association, *Monitor on Psychology* (July/August 2004, Vol 35, No. 7), https://www.apa.org/monitor/julaug04/standing

13. "Height and intelligence", *Wikipedia* (24 April, 2024), https://en.wikipedia.org/wiki/ Height_and_intelligence#Statistics

14. Reuters, "Taller people are smarter, too, study says", *NBC News* (August 25, 2006), https://www.nbcnews.com/id/wbna14517687

15. Rob Henderson, "5 Reasons Why Women and Men Care About Height", *Psychology Today* (September 24, 2019), https://www.psychologytoday.com/za/blog/ after-service/201909/ 5-reasons-why-women-and-men-care-about-height

16. Cher Gopman and Hannah Madden, "Why Do Girls like Tall Boys? 12 Explanations", *WikiHow* (Updated January 31, 2024), https://www.wikihow.com/Why-Do-Women-Like-Tall-Men

17. Daily Mail Reporter, "The height of romance: Women want partners who are 8in taller than them but men prefer a gap of just 3in", *Daily Mail* (17 February, 2013), https://www.dailymail.co.uk/news/article-2279945/The-height-romance-Women-want-partners-8in-taller-men-prefer-gap-just-3in.html

18. Irmina Salska, David A. Frederick, Boguslaw Pawlowski, Andrew H. Reilly, Kelsey T. Laird, Nancy A. Rudd, "Conditional mate preferences: Factors influencing preferences for height", *Personality and Individual Differences* (Volume 44, Issue 1), 2008, Pages 203-215, ISSN 0191-8869, https://doi.org/10.1016/j.paid.2007.08.008. (https://www.sciencedirect.com/science/article/pii/S0191886907002814)

19. Raven Saunt, " 'Dating is almost impossible': Woman who was bullied for being 6ft 2in tall speaks out about her struggle of finding a boyfriend", *Daily Mail* (10 April, 2023), https://www.dailymail.co.uk/femail/article-11956871/Im-6ft-2in-woman-dating-impossible.html

20. Riceman, "Would You Date a Tall Girl? Social Experiment",

YouTube (August 30, 2021),
https://www.youtube.com/watch?v=IL0eoTHOGPo

21. eHarmony Editorial Team, "Dating a Short Guy – Why True Love Goes Beyond Physical Attraction", *eharmony* (April 12, 2021), https://www.eharmony.com/dating-advice/finding-yourself/dating-a-short-guy/

22. T. Joel Wade, Rebecca Burch, Maryanne L. Fisher, Haley Casper, "On a pedestal: High heels and the perceived attractiveness and evolutionary fitness of women", *Personality and Individual Differences*, (Volume 188, 2022), 111456, ISSN 0191-8869, https://doi.org/10.1016/j.paid.2021.111456. (https://www.sciencedirect.com/science/article/pii/S0191886921008357)

23. "5 Reasons High Heels Make Women Look More Attractive", *Enrico Cuini*, https://www.enricocuini.com/blog/5-reasons-high-heels-make-women-look-more-attractive

24. Laura Williams, "12 Struggles Tall Women Deal With", *The List* (February 9, 2017), https://www.thelist.com/41186/12-struggles-tall-women-deal/

25. "Average human height by country", *Wikipedia* (24 April, 2024), https://en.wikipedia.org/wiki/Average_human_height_by_country

CHAPTER 3: Weight

1. "Overweight",
   Wikipedia (25 April, 2024),
   https://en.wikipedia.org/wiki/Overweight

2. "Why do women have a greater risk of obesity compared to men?",
   Medical Academic,
   https://www.medicalacademic.co.za/endocrinology/why-do-women-have-a-greater-risk-of-obesity-compared-to-men.

3. "Feminine beauty ideal",
   Wikipedia (25 April, 2024),
   https://en.wikipedia.org/wiki/Feminine_beauty_ideal

4. "Masculinity",
   Wikipedia (25 April, 2024),
   https://en.wikipedia.org/wiki/Masculinity

5. Viren Swami, "Women's idealised bodies have changed dramatically over time – but are standards becoming more unattainable?",
   The Conversation (September 13, 1016),
   https://theconversation.com/womens-idealised-bodies-have-changed-dramatically-over-time-but-are-standards-becoming-more-unattainable-64936

6. Kelly King and Rebecca Puhl, "Weight Bias: Does it Affect Men and Women Differently?",
   Obesity Action Coalition (Spring 2013),

https://www.obesityaction.org/resources/weight-bias
-does-it-affect-men-and-women-differently/

7. Voges Mona M. , Giabbiconi Claire-Marie , Schöne
Benjamin , Waldorf Manuel , Hartmann Andrea S. ,
Vocks Silja, "Gender Differences in Body Evaluation:
Do Men Show More Self-Serving Double Standards
Than Women?"
Frontiers in Psychology (Vol 10, 2019), DOI 10.3389/
fpsyg.2019.00544, ISSN=1664-1078,
https://www.frontiersin.org/journals/psychology/
articles/10.3389/fpsyg.2019.00544

8. "OVERWEIGHT AND OBESITY: Causes and Risk
Factors",
National Heart, Lung and Blood Institute (updated
March 24, 2022),
https://www.nhlbi.nih.gov/health/overweight-and-
obesity/causes

9. University of Illinois College of Agricultural, Consumer
and Environmental Sciences (ACES), "Who's to blame
for obesity? Policy makers, the food industry, or individuals?"
ScienceDaily (22 January 2014),
https://www.sciencedaily.com/releases/2014/01/14012
2112422.htm

10. "Educate medics about weight stigma to reduce UK's
obesity rate",
UCL News (10 August, 2022),
https://www.ucl.ac.uk/news/2022/aug/educate-
medics-about-weight-stigma-reduce-uks-

obesity-rate

11. Brewis, Alexandra A., et al. "Body Norms and Fat Stigma in Global Perspective." *Current Anthropology* (vol. 52, no. 2), 2011, pp. 269–76. *JSTOR*, https://doi.org/10.1086/659309. Accessed 26 Mar. 2024.

12. Judith J. Wurtman, "Being Overweight: Who Is To Blame?", *Psychology Today* (April 3, 2011), https://www.psychologytoday.com/za/blog/the-antidepressant-diet/201104/being-overweight-who-is-blame

13. RTS (Radio Télévision Suisse), "Grossophobie: Dans la tête d'un gros", *YouTube* (July 23, 2018), https://www.youtube.com/watch?v=NHu2nFv0CfU

14. Lisa Quast, "Thin Is In For Executive Women: How Weight Discrimination Contributes To The Glass Ceiling.", *Forbes* (August 6, 2012), https://www.forbes.com/sites/lisaquast/2012/08/06/thin-is-in-for-executive-women-as-weight-discrimination-contributes-to-glass-ceiling

15. Michigan State University, "Weight bias plagues U.S. elections", *MSU Today* (May 19, 2014), https://msutoday.msu.edu/news/2014/weight-bias-plagues-us-elections

16. Eliana Dockterman, "How a Female Political Candidate's Looks Affect Her Ability to Win",
Time (May 20, 2014),
https://time.com/106145/how-a-female-political-candidates-looks-affect-her-ability-to-win/

17. Isabel Wilkinson, "France's Chic New Women Cabinet Members",
The Daily Beast (updated July 13, 2017),
https://www.thedailybeast.com/frances-chic-new-women-cabinet-members

18. UCLA Anderson, "Employees Subtly Discriminate",
YouTube (July 28, 2016),
https://www.youtube.com/watch?v=XxBVpXX9i74

19. Virgie Tovar, "What It's Really Like to Date as a Fat Woman",
Good Housekeeping (updated February 4, 2022),
https://www.goodhousekeeping.com/life/relationships/a35730257/plus-size-dating/

20. "Obesity",
World Health Organisation,
https://www.who.int/data/gho/indicator-metadata-registry/imr-details/3420.

CHAPTER 4: Gender

1. Bartley EJ, Fillingim RB. "Sex differences in pain: a brief review of clinical and experimental findings". Br J Anaesth. 2013 Jul;111(1):52-8. doi: 10.1093/bja/aet 127. PMID: 23794645; PMCID: PMC3690315. https://www.ncbi.nlm.nih.gov/pmc/articles/PMC3690

315/

2. "Cold Wars: Why Women Feel The Chill More",
Pfizer,
https://www.pfizer.com/news/articles/cold_wars_
why_women_feel_the_chill_more

3. Natalie Wolchover, "Men vs. Women: Our Key Physical Differences Explained",
Live Science (September 22, 2011),
https://www.livescience.com/33513-men-vs-women
-our-physical-differences-explained.html

4. "Sex differences in psychology",
Wikipedia (23 April, 2024),
https://en.wikipedia.org/wiki/Sex_differences_in_
psychology#Behavior

5. Thomas F. Denson, Siobhan M. O'Dean, Khandis R. Blake, Joanne R. Beames, "Aggression in Women: Behavior, Brain and Hormones",
Frontiers in Behavioural Neuroscience (02 May, 2018),
https://www.frontiersin.org/articles/10.3389/fnbeh.20
18.00081/full

6. Joseph H. Manson, "Why Are Women More Fearful Than Men?",
The Society for Personality and Social Psychology (June 24, 2022),
https://spsp.org/news/character-and-context-blog/
manson-women-more-fearful

7. "The Difference Between Alcoholic Men and Women",
Experience Recovery,

https://www.experiencerecovery.com/blog/
men-women-alcoholic-difference/

8. Barriga, Alvaro Q., Elizabeth M. Morrison, Albert K.
Liau, and John C. Gibbs. "Moral Cognition: Explaining
the Gender Difference in Antisocial Behavior."
Merrill-Palmer Quarterly 47, no. 4 (2001): 532–62.
http://www.jstor.org/stable/23093698

9. Rick Sarre, Andrew Day, Ben Livings, Catia Malvaso,
"Men are more likely to commit violent crimes. Why is
this so and how do we change it?",
The Conversation (March 26, 2021),
https://theconversation.com/men-are-more-likely-to
-commit-violent-crimes-why-is-this-so-and-how-do
-we-change-it-157331

10. "Incarceration rates by country 2024",
World Population Review,
https://worldpopulationreview.com/country-rankings
/incarceration-rates-by-country

11. Alix Capper Murdoch, "Unravelling the statistics: Are
men better drivers than women?",
The National News (February 27, 2020),
https://www.thenationalnews.com/lifestyle/motor-
ing/unravelling-the-statistics-are-men-better-
drivers-than-women-1.985365

12. "Road-traffic injuries",
World Health Organisation (13 December, 2023),
https://www.who.int/news-room/fact-sheets/detail/
road-traffic-injuries

13. Mayo Clinic Staff, "Depression in women: Understanding the gender gap",
Mayo Clinic (January 29, 2019),
https://www.mayoclinic.org/diseases-conditions/depression/in-depth/depression/art-20047725

14. "Sex differences in leadership",
Wikipedia (23 April, 2024),
https://en.wikipedia.org/wiki/Sex_differences_in_leadership

15. Lisa Burden, "HR is overwhelmingly white and female, data indicates",
HR Dive (February 20, 2019),
https://www.hrdive.com/news/hr-is-overwhelmingly-white-and-female-data-indicates/548600/

16. Ilina Joshi, "The Domination of Women in Public Relations",
The Women's Network (March 10, 2022),
https://www.thewomens.network/blog/the-domination-of-women-in-public-relations

17. Catherine Ferraro, George Mason University, "Study finds 'masculine' women get more promotions at work",
Phys.Org (January 27, 2011),
https://phys.org/news/2011-01-masculine-women.html

18. Helena Dalli, "The best man in the Cabinet",
Times of Malta (April 15, 2013),
https://timesofmalta.com/article/The-best-man-in-the-Cabinet.465651

19. Chloe Lane, "Why Are Female Students Choosing to Study Courses With a Lower Earning Potential?", *Top Universities* (updated March 23, 2021), https://www.topuniversities.com/student-info/university-news/why-are-female-students-choosing-study-courses-lower-earning-potential

20. Laura Greaves, "Key trends among STEM graduates", *Prospects Luminate* (June 2019), https://luminate.prospects.ac.uk/key-trends-among-stem-graduates

21. Arun Advani, Sarah Smith, Ben Waltmann, Xiaowei Xu, "Gender differences in subject choice leads to gender pay gap immediately after graduation", *Institute for Fiscal Studies* (4 October, 2021), https://ifs.org.uk/articles/gender-differences-subject-choice-leads-gender-pay-gap-immediately-after-graduation

22. WIN Team, "Gender Equality Paradox: Study Says Biology Determines a Person's Career Choice", *Collective for Equality* (February 14, 2022), https://collectiveforequality.com/gender-equality-paradox-biology-determines-persons-career-choice/

23. "Gender-equality paradox", *Wikipedia* (23 April, 2024), https://en.wikipedia.org/wiki/Gender-equality_paradox

24. "Plumber demographics and statistics in the US", *Zippia*, https://www.zippia.com/plumber-jobs/demographics/

25. "Data Spotlight: Men In Nursing: Five-Year Trends Show No Growth",
American Association of Colleges of Nursing (April 3, 2023)
https://www.aacnnursing.org/news-data/all-news/data
-spotlight-men-in-nursing-five-year-trends-show-no
-growth

26. "Body-builder apprentice demographics and statistics in the US",
Zippia,
https://www.zippia.com/body-builder-apprentice-
jobs/demographics/

27. Madison Freeman, "In a field where the patient demographic is dominated by women, why are most plastic surgeons men?",
American Society of Plastic Surgeons (March 31, 2023),
https://www.plasticsurgery.org/news/articles/in-a-
field-where-the-patient-demographic-is-dominated-
by-women-why-are-most-plastic-surgeons-men

28. BraveTheWorld, "50 Real Differences Between Men & Women",
YouTube (August 19, 2016),
https://www.youtube.com/watch?v=yhwO8u4sZ-8

29. Bruce Goldman, "Two minds: The cognitive differences between men and women",
Standford Medicine Magazine: Neurobiology (May 22, 2017),
https://stanmed.stanford.edu/how-mens-and-womens
-brains-are-different/

30. Elayne Boosler Quotes. (n.d.).
BrainyQuote.com. Retrieved April 18, 2024, from
BrainyQuote.com Web site:
https://brainyquote.com/quotes/elayne_boosler_
136565

31. Kim Parker, Juliana Menasce Horowitz, Renee Stepler,
"On Gender Differences, No Consensus on Nature vs.
Nurture",
Pew Research Center (December 5, 2017),
https://www.pewresearch.org/social-trends/2017/12/0
5/on-gender-differences-no-consensus-on-nature-vs
-nurture/

32. Ibid.

CHAPTER 5: Age

1. Clara De Paula Couto, Ronja Ostermeier, Klaus
Rothermund, "Age Differences in Age Stereotypes",
GeroPsych (August 19, 2021),
https://econtent.hogrefe.com/doi/10.1024/1662-9647/
a000272#

2. "Youth violence",
World Health Organisation (11 October, 2023),
https://www.who.int/news-room/fact-sheets/detail/
youth-violence#

3. "Ageism",
Wikipedia (24 April, 2024),
https://en.wikipedia.org/wiki/Ageism

4. Francioli SP, North MS. "Youngism: The content, caus-

es, and consequences of prejudices toward younger adults." *J Exp Psychol Gen.* 2021 Dec;150(12):2591-2612. doi: 10.1037/xge0001064. Epub 2021 Aug 19. PMID: 34410803. https://pubmed.ncbi.nlm.nih.gov/34410803/#

5. Jessenia Mota, "Is 'Youngism' the new ageism (and what are you doing about it?)", *TLNT* (April 12, 2022), https://www.tlnt.com/articles/is-youngism-the-new-a geism-and-what-are-you-doing-about-it

6. Jonathan Haidt and Pamela Paresky, "By mollycoddling our children, we're fuelling mental illness in teenagers", *The Guardian* (10 January, 2019), https://www.theguardian.com/commentisfree/2019/ jan/10/by-mollycoddling-our-children-were-fuelling-mental-illness-in-teenagers

7. "Millennials: The Me Me Me Generation", *Time* (May 20, 2013), https://time.com/247/millennials-the-me-me-me-generation/

8. Simon Sinek, "The video on millennials in the workplace that everyone must watch", *New York Post* (September 30, 2017), https://nypost.com/2017/09/30/this-15-minute-speech -helps-explain-millennials-in-the-workplace/

9. "Si jeunesse savait, si vieillesse pouvait", *Wiktionary* (24 April, 2024), https://en.wiktionary.org/wiki/si_jeunesse_savait,

_si_vieillesse_pouvait

10. Dustin Hawley, "How Old Do You Have To Be To Rent a Car?",
    JD Power (March 15, 2021),
    https://www.jdpower.com/cars/shopping-guides/how
    -old-do-you-have-to-be-to-rent-a-car#

11. Steven Glass, "Average Car Insurance Rates by Age and Gender: Everything You Need to Know",
    Car and Driver (November 2, 2023),
    https://www.caranddriver.com/car-insurance/a361640
    61/average-car-insurance-rates-by-age-and-gender/

12. Kate Morgan, "Why inexperienced workers can't get entry-level jobs",
    BBC (20 September, 2021),
    https://www.bbc.com/worklife/article/20210916-why
    -inexperienced-workers-cant-get-entry-level-jobs

13. Clare Mehta, "Forget your 20s, it's your 30s when you hit the happiness sweet spot",
    The Sydney Morning Herald (April 13, 2021),
    https://www.smh.com.au/lifestyle/life-and-
    relationships/forget-your-20s-it-s-your-30s-
    when-you-hit-the-happiness-sweet-spot-
    20210412-p57idb.html

14. Berger, R. (2017), "Aging in America: Ageism and General Attitudes toward Growing Old and the Elderly",
    Open Journal of Social Sciences, **5**, 183-198, DOI 10.4236/jss.2017.58015.,
    https://www.scirp.org/journal/
    paperinformation?paperid=78445

15. John Williamson '64 and Tay McNamara "Reframing ageism",
MIT Technology Review (April 25, 2023),
https://www.technologyreview.com/
2023/04/25/1070410/reframing-ageism/

16. Dale Archer, "Forever Young: America's Obsession With Never Growing Old",
Psychology Today (October 2, 2013),
https://www.psychologytoday.com/intl/blog/
reading-between-the-headlines/201310/forever-young-americas-obsession-never-growing-old

17. Sheila Callaham, "Accused Of Excluding Older Applicants, Eli Lilly Settles Again",
Forbes (August 27, 2023),
https://www.forbes.com/sites/sheilacallaham/2023/08
/27/accused-of-excluding-older-applicants-eli-lilly-settles-again/

18. Susan Pickard, "Last love: The 'double standard of ageing' and women's experience of gender and sexuality at mid-life",
Journal of Aging Studies (Volume 60, 2022), 100989,
ISSN 0890-4065,
https://doi.org/10.1016/j.jaging.2021.100989

19. Andrea Mandell, "Where are real portrayals of women over 50 on screen? New study highlights dearth of leading roles",
USA Today (October 27, 2020),
https://www.usatoday.com/story/entertainment/
movies/2020/10/27/women-over-50-losing-out-

major-movie-roles-study-finds/6048202002/

20. De Pater, I. E., Judge, T. A., & Scott, B. A. (2014). "Age, Gender, and Compensation: A Study of Hollywood Movie Stars." *Journal of Management Inquiry*, 23(4), 407-420. https://doi.org/10.1177/1056492613519861

21. George Burns Quotes. (n.d.). *BrainyQuote.com*. Retrieved April 18, 2024, from BrainyQuote.com Web site: https://brainyquote.com/quotes/george_burns_150284

CHAPTER 6: Face

1. "Physiognomy", *Wikipedia* (25 April, 2024), https://en.wikipedia.org/wiki/Physiognomy#Scientific_investigation

2. Ibid.

3. Melanie Hearse, "Are you better off with a pretty face, or a friendly one?", *news.com.au* (March 8, 2017), https://www.news.com.au/lifestyle/beauty/face-body/are-you-better-off-with-a-pretty-face-or-a-friendly-one/news-story/392d0a777bc18d997f9344753cce373c

4. Groucho Marx Quotes. (n.d.). *BrainyQuote.com*. Retrieved March 27, 2024, from BrainyQuote.com Web site:

https://brainyquote.com/quotes/groucho_marx_
128205

5. Goldstein, A.G., Chance, J.E. & Gilbert, B., "Facial stereotypes of good guys and bad guys: A replication and extension.",
Bull. Psychon. Soc. **22**, 549-552 (1984).
https://doi.org/10.3758/BF03333904

6. "Physiognomy",
Wikipedia (25 April, 2024),
https://en.wikipedia.org/wiki/Physiognomy#Scientific
_investigation

7. "Physiognomy",
Wikipedia (3 May, 2024),
https://en.wikipedia.org/wiki/Physiognomy

8. Jesse Emspak, "Facing Facts: Artificial Intelligence and the Resurgence of Physiognomy",
Undark (11.08.2017),
https://undark.org/2017/11/08/facing-facts-artificial-intelligence/

9. "Facial Recognition in Healthcare: Unlocking Potential Medical Applications",
Alchera (August 14, 2023),
https://alchera.ai/en/meet-alchera/blog/facial-recognition-in-healthcare-unlocking-potential-medical-applications

10. Kachur. A., Osin, E., Davydov, D. *et al.* "Assessing the Big Five personality traits using real-life static facial images.",

Sci Rep **10**, 8487 (2020).
https://doi.org/10.1038/s41598-020-65358-6

11. Newsroom, "AI can predict person's politics by their looks and smile",
Modern Diplomacy (July 3, 2023), July 3, 2023,
https://moderndiplomacy.eu/2023/07/03/ai-can-predict-persons-politics-by-their-looks-and-smile/

12. Deann Gayman-Unl, "Expressive faces predict who's liberal or conservative",
Futurity (April 5, 2018),
https://www.futurity.org/liberals-conservatives-facial-expressions-1723472-2/

13. Kosinski, M. "Facial recognition technology can expose political orientation from naturalistic facial images.",
Sci Rep **11**, 100 (2021).
https://doi.org/10.1038/s41598-020-79310-1

14. Chad Boutin, "To determine election outcomes, study says snap judgments are sufficient",
Princeton University (Oct 22, 2007),
https://www.princeton.edu/news/2007/10/22/determine-election-outcomes-study-says-snap-judgments-are-sufficient

CHAPTER 7: Attire
1. Barry Samaha and Shelby Ying Hyde, "The Best Coco Chanel Quotes About Fashion, Love, and Success",
Harper's Bazaar (July 7, 2021),
https://www.harpersbazaar.com/fashion/designers/

g32971271/best-coco-chanel-quotes/

2. Charles Kelso, "The Psychology of Dressing Well: How
   Formal Clothing Boosts Confidence and Perception",
   Bondeno (September 9, 2023),
   https://www.bondenoshoes.com/blogs/
   bespoke-shoe-blog/the-psychology-of-dressing-
   well-how-formal-clothing-boosts-
   confidence-and-perception?

3. Oscar Wilde,
   Quotefancy,
   https://quotefancy.com/quote/287/Oscar-Wilde-You-
   can-never-be-overdressed-or-overeducated

4. Carmen Lopez, "Look good, feel great: the psychology
   of clothing",
   Current Boutique,
   https://currentboutique.com/blogs/cravingcurrent/
   psychology-of-clothing

5. Kendra Cherry, "Color Psychology: Does It Affect How
   You Feel?",
   Very Well Mind (updated February 20, 2024),
   https://www.verywellmind.com/color-psychology-
   2795824

6. Stephen Orbanek, "Temple study suggests dressing
   your best improves workplace productivity",
   Temple Now (1 June 2023),
   https://news.temple.edu/news/2023-06-01/when-
   you-look-good-you-feel-good-research-shows-you-
   might-even-be-more-productive

7. "Deposition Benefits of Witnesses Dressing Professionally",
Casamo & Associates,
https://www.casamo.com/deposition-benefits-of-witnesses-dressing-professionally

8. Vanessa Van Edwards, "Fashion Psychology: What Your Choice in Clothes Says About You",
Science of People,
https://www.scienceofpeople.com/fashion-psychology/

9. Jacquelyn Smith, "Steve Jobs Always Dressed Exactly the Same. Here's Who Else Does.",
Forbes (October 5, 2012),
https://www.forbes.com/sites/jacquelynsmith/2012/10/05/steve-jobs-always-dressed-exactly-the-same-heres-who-else-does

10. Drake Baer, "Always Wear The Same Suit: Obama's Presidential Productivity Secrets",
Fast Company (02-12-14),
https://www.fastcompany.com/3026265/always-wear-the-same-suit-obamas-presidential-productivity-secrets

11. Monique Younès, "Emmanuel Macron: comment son look est devenu une partie intégrante de sa communication",
RTL (14/05/2022),
https://www.rtl.fr/actu/politique/emmanuel-macron-comment-son-look-est-devenu-une-partie-integrante-de-sa-communication-7900153865

12. Aubrey Martin, "Why Women Take So Long To Get Ready,"
Odyssey (August 8, 2016),
https://www.theodysseyonline.com/women-take-long-ready

13. Moody, Wendy & Kinderman, Peter & Sinha, Pammi, "An exploratory study: Relationships between trying on clothing, mood, emotion, personality and clothing preference."
Journal of Fashion Marketing and Management (March 2010). 14. 161-179. 10.1108/13612021011025483.,
https://www.researchgate.net/publication/235271563_An_exploratory_study_Relationships_between_trying_on_clothing_mood_emotion_personality_and_clothing_preference

14. Jamie Lower, University of Central Florida, "Style Speaks: Clothing Judgments, Gender Stereotypes, and Expectancy Violations of Professional Women", (2018), *Electronic Theses and Dissertations. 5785.*
https://stars.library.ucf.edu/etd/5785

CHAPTER 8: Demeanour

1. Melanie Hearse, "Are you better off with a pretty face, or a friendly one?",
news.com.au (March 8, 2017),
https://www.news.com.au/lifestyle/beauty/face-body/are-you-better-off-with-a-pretty-face-or-a-friendly-one/news-story/392d0a777bc18d997f9344753cce373c

2. Michael Booth,
The Almost Nearly Perfect People (London: Vintage, 2015), p. 313

3. "Columbo",
Wikipedia (25 April, 2024),
https://en.wikipedia.org/wiki/Columbo

4. Maria Dinzeo, "Judge Orders Transparent Masks for Witnesses in Criminal Trial",
Courthouse News Service (July 16, 2020),
https://www.courthousenews.com/judge-orders-transparent-masks-for-witnesses-in-criminal-trial/

5. Laurie L. Levenson, "Courtroom Demeanour: The Theater of the Courtroom",
Minnesota Law Review (2008),
https://scholarship.law.umn.edu/cgi/viewcontent.cgi?article=1581&context=mlr#:

6. Rajneesh Mittal, "Unveiling the Power of Body Language and Attitude in Job Interviews: Beyond Technical Skills",
LinkedIn (January 11, 2024),
https://www.linkedin.com/pulse/unveiling-power-body-language-attitude-job-interviews-rajneesh-mittal-vvabc/?trk=article-ssr-frontend-pulse_more-articles_related-content-card

CHAPTER 9: Voice

1. "Linguistic profiling",
Wikipedia (25 April, 2024),
https://en.wikipedia.org/wiki/Linguistic_profiling

2. Bright Side, "What Your Voice Reveals About You",
YouTube (October 3, 2019),
https://www.youtube.com/
watch?v=SM0Evtrrodg&t=483s

3. University of Gottingen, "What Does Your Voice Say
About You? Study Links Personality Traits To Voice
Characteristics",
Neuroscience News (May 14, 2021),
https://neurosciencenews.com/personality-voice-184
27/

4. The Editors, "James Earl Jones",
Encyclopaedia Britannica (March 18, 2024),
https://www.britannica.com/biography/
James-Earl-Jones

5. Allie Nelson, "Morgan Freeman's Net Worth In 2024
Includes Several Million Dollars, Baby",
Parade (updated January 11, 2024),
https://parade.com/celebrities/
morgan-freeman-net-worth

6. "African-American vernacular English",
Wikipedia (25 April, 2024),
https://en.wikipedia.org/wiki/
African-American_Vernacular_English

7. Kurinec CA, Weaver CA 3rd. " 'Sounding Black':
Speech Stereotypicality Activates Racial Stereotypes
and Expectations About Appearance."
Front Psychol. (2021 Dec 24);12:785283. doi: 10.
3389/fpsyg.2021.785283. PMID: 35002876; PMCID:
PMC8740186,

https://www.ncbi.nlm.nih.gov/pmc/articles/
PMC8740186/

8. Abbie MacNeal, Katherine Fiallo, Alexander Jones,
Shaughnessy Jones, Samantha Laureano, Matthew
Monjarrez, Yian Xu, " 'Sounding Black': The Legal Im-
plications of Linguistic Profiling",
*Northeastern University, NEU Working Papers in Lin-
guistics* (2019), Vol. 4,
h t t p s : // r e p o s i t o r y . l i b r a r y . n o r t h e a s t -
ern.edu/files/neu:m046pb24z
(chrome-extension://efaidnbmnnnibpcajpcglclefindm
kaj/https://repository.library.northeastern.edu/downlo
ads/neu:m046pb27s?datastream_id=content)

9. "Linguistic profiling",
Wikipedia (25 April, 2024),
https://en.wikipedia.org/wiki/
Linguistic_profiling#In_institutions

10. Godfrey Edward Arnold, "Speech: Vocal attributes",
Britannica (25 April, 2024),
https://www.britannica.com/topic/
speech-language/Vocal-attributes

11. Alex Peters, "Unspoken phenomenon: why women are
deepening their voices in the workplace",
Dazed Digital (10 March 2022),
https://www.dazeddigital.com/beauty/article/55558/1/
unspoken-phenomenon-why-women-are-
deepening-their-voices-in-the-workplace

12. Annika Hope, "The Vocal Differences Between The
Genders",

Music Gateway (8.2.2023),
https://www.musicgateway.com/blog/how-to/
the-vocal-differences-between-genders

13. "Male vs. female voiceovers",
Sheffield,
https://www.sheffieldav.com/education/
male-vs-female-voiceovers#

14. "Voiceover styles",
Voicecrafters,
https://www.voicecrafters.com/style/

15. "I Have a Dream",
Wikipedia (25 April, 2024),
https://en.wikipedia.org/wiki/I_Have_a_Dream

CHAPTER 10: Accent

1. Frenchly, "Parisians Try to Pronounce Words in English",
YouTube (June 4, 2019),
https://www.youtube.com/watch?v=uy2LRxdlgWA

2. Paola Peralta, "5 regional accents applicants hide in job interviews",
Employee Benefit News (May 22, 2023),
https://www.benefitnews.com/list/applicants-with-
these-5-accents-hide-them-in-interviews

3. "Regional accents are a bar to legal careers, researchers find",
De Montfort University (30 January, 2023),
https://www.dmu.ac.uk/about-dmu/news/2023/

january/regional-accents-are-a-bar-to-legal-careers-researchers-find.aspx

4. Janice Gassam Asare, "Accent Discrimination Is Still A Pervasive Issue In The Workplace, Research Finds", *Forbes* (November 18, 2022), https://www.forbes.com/sites/janicegassam/2022/11/18/accent-discrimination-is-still-a-pervasive-issue-in-the-workplace-research-finds

5. Peter Yeung, "In France, Accents Are Now Protected by Law", *Reasons to be cheerful* (April 2, 2021), https://reasonstobecheerful.world/glottophobia-accent-discrimination-france/

6. Marine Le Breton, "Ce qui se cache derrière les moqueries sur les accents, la glottophobie", *HuffPost* (26/11/2020), https://www.huffingtonpost.fr/life/article/ce-qui-se-cache-derriere-les-moqueries-sur-les-accents-la-glottophobie_173248.html

7. Gerry Howley, "Why do some accents sound better than others?", *The Conversation* (May 15, 2017), https://theconversation.com/why-do-some-accents-sound-better-than-others-77732

8. https://www.movieflavor.com/

9. "Why Do We Find the British Accent So Charming?" *Go localise*, https://golocalise.com/blog/why-do-we-find-the-

british-accent-so-charming

10. Destiny Uteh, "Must Watch For Black People – Perks Of British Accent In America", *YouTube* (August 31, 2022), https://www.youtube.com/watch?v=Z7VpGl-JqVA&t=39s

11. Michael Erard, "The reason you discriminate against foreign accents starts with what they do to your brain", *Quartz* (February 25, 2016), https://qz.com/624335/the-reason-you-discriminate-against-foreign-accents-starts-with-what-they-do-to-your-brain#

12. Kinzler KD, Dupoux E, Spelke ES. "The native language of social cognition" *Proc Natl Acad Sci U S A*. 2007 Jul 24; 104(30):12577-80. doi: 10.1073/pnas.0705345104. Epub 2007 Jul 17. PMID: 17640881; PMCID: PMC1941511. https://www.ncbi.nlm.nih.gov/pmc/articles/PMC1941511/

13. Richard Gray, "Why do people discriminate against speakers with foreign accents?", *Horizon magazine* (21 January 2019), https://projects.research-and-innovation.ec.europa.eu/en/horizon-magazine/why-do-people-discriminate-against-speakers-foreign-accents

14. "Standard German", *Wikipedia* (26 April, 2024), https://en.wikipedia.org/wiki/Standard_German

15. "My Fair Lady (film)",
Wikipedia (26 April, 2024),
https://en.wikipedia.org/wiki/My_Fair_Lady_(film)

CHAPTER 11: Name

1. William Shakespeare, "Romeo and Juliet: Act 2,
Scene 2",
My Shakespeare,
https://myshakespeare.com/romeo-and-juliet/
act-2-scene-2

2. Dave Chesson, "Great Character Name Generator
Sites [2024] + Character Naming Tips",
Kindlepreneur (January 8, 2024),
https://kindlepreneur.com/character-name-
generator/

3. Angus Chen, "Your Name Might Shape Your Face, Researchers Say",
NPR (February 27, 2017),
https://www.npr.org/sections/health-shots/
2017/02/27/517496915/your-name-might-
shape-your-face-researchers-say

4. Holly Yan, "Female hurricanes are deadlier than male
hurricanes, study says",
CNN (Sept 1, 2016),
https://edition.cnn.com/2016/09/01/health/
female-hurricanes-deadlier-than-male-hurricanes-
trnd/index.html

5. Kevin Keating, "What's In a Name? The Science behind Product Naming",

PKG Brand Design,
https://www.pkgbranding.com/blog/
whats-in-a-name-the-science-behind-
product-naming

6. "Boeing 737 MAX",
   Wikipedia (26 April, 2024),
   https://en.wikipedia.org/wiki/Boeing_737_MAX

7. Pete Muntean, Gregory Wallace and Chris Isidore,
   "Key bolts were missing from a Boeing door plug that
   blew out in mid-air, report says",
   CNN (February 7, 2024),
   https://edition.cnn.com/2024/02/06/business/ntsb-
   boeing-alaska-door-plug-blowout-faa/index.html#

8. "Edsel",
   Wikipedia (26 April, 2024),
   https://en.wikipedia.org/wiki/Edsel

9. Marianne Bertrand, "This Problem Has a Name: Discrimination",
   Chicago Booth Review (May 21, 2016),
   https://www.chicagobooth.edu/review/
   problem-has-name-discrimination

10. Sean Fath, "When Blind Hiring Advances DEI – and
    When It Doesn't",
    Harvard Business Review (June 01, 2023),
    https://hbr.org/2023/06/when-blind-hiring-
    advances-dei-and-when-it-doesnt#

11. Pragnesh Anekal, "8 Surprising Blind Hiring Statistics",
    Adaface (February 08, 2023),

https://www.adaface.com/blog/blind-hiring-statistics/

CHAPTER 12: Job

1. Ogden Nash Quotes. (n.d.).
BrainyQuote.com. Retrieved March 29, 2024, from
BrainyQuote.com Web site:
https://brainyquote.com/quotes/ogden_nash_134718

2. Shawn Gold, "Is Creativity Inherently Liberal?",
LinkedIn (October 11, 2021),
https://www.linkedin.com/pulse/creativity-
inherently-liberal-shawn-gold/

3. Bite-sized Philosophy, "Jordan Peterson – IQ and the
Job Market",
YouTube (April 19, 2017),
https://www.youtube.com/
watch?v=fjs2gPa5sD0&t=148s

4. Tom Huddleston Jr., "Top psychologist: IQ is the No. 1
predictor of work success – especially combined with
these 5 traits",
CNBC (June 11, 2022),
https://www.cnbc.com/2022/07/11/does-iq-
determine-success-a-psychologist-weighs-in.html

5. "Intelligence and public policy,"
Wikipedia (26 April, 2024),
https://en.wikipedia.org/wiki/Intelligence_and_
public_policy#US_military_service

6. Official IQ Test, "Genius IQ Score: Unraveling the Secrets of Exceptional Intelligence",

LinkedIn (April 23, 2023),
https://www.linkedin.com/pulse/genius-iq-score-unraveling-secrets-exceptional-intelligence/

7. Rich Karlgaard, "The Trillion Dollar IQ Business",
Forbes (September 7, 2010),
https://www.forbes.com/sites/richkarlgaard/2010/09/07/the-trillion-dollar-iq-business

8. Judith Akoyi, "Genius Behind the Brand: Analyzing the IQ of Steve Jobs and Its Influence on Apple's Success",
brainmanager.io (31 May, 2024),
https://brainmanager.io/blog/cognitive/what-is-steve-jobs-iq

9. Linda Geddes, "The truth about intelligence: What makes someone smarter than others?",
New Scientist (18 July, 2018),
https://www.newscientist.com/article/mg23931870-500-the-truth-about-intelligence-what-makes-someone-smarter-than-others

10. Ibid.

11. Jacques Buffett, "Top Most Respected Jobs 2022",
Zety (August 23, 2023),
https://zety.com/blog/most-respected-jobs

12. Johnny Wood, "10 most respected professions in the world",
World Economic Forum (January 15, 2019),
https://www.weforum.org/agenda/2019/01/most-respected-professions-in-the-world

13. Jonason, P.K., Thomas, A.G., "Being More Educated

and Earning More Increases Romantic Interest: Data
from 1.8 M Online Daters from 24 Nations."
Hum Nat **33**, 115-131 (2022).
https://doi.org/10.1007/s12110-022-09422-2

14. "Hypergamy",
    Wikipedia (26 April, 2024),
    https://en.wikipedia.org/wiki/Hypergamy#Research

15. Jérôme Adda (Università Bocconi), Christian Dust-
    mann (University College London and Center for Re-
    search and Analysis of Migration), Katrien Stevens
    (University of Sydney), "The career cost of children:
    career and fertility trade-offs)",
    Microeconomic Insights (27 June, 2018),
    https://microeconomicinsights.org/career-cost-
    children-career-fertility-trade-offs/

16. David Mielach, "75 Percent of Women Say They Won't
    Date Unemployed Men",
    yahoo!news (June 27, 2012),
    https://www.yahoo.com/news/75-percent-women-
    wont-date-unemployed-men-113858283.html?

17. "Hypergamy",
    Wikipedia (26 April, 2024),
    https://en.wikipedia.org/wiki/Hypergamy#Research

18. Suzanne Venker, "Why super-successful women strug-
    gle in love",
    Washington Examiner (October 9, 2019),
    https://www.washingtonexaminer.com/opinion/18235
    75/why-super-successful-women-struggle-in-love/

19. Soulaima Gourani, "Why Are Men So Intimidated By Successful Women?",
Swaay (28 February, 2020),
https://swaay.com/men-intimidated-successful-women

20. Stephanie Linning, "Tinder reveals the most right-swiped jobs around the world – so could YOUR career help you find love?",
Daily Mail (5 September, 2018),
https://www.dailymail.co.uk/femail/article-6134747/Tinder-reveals-right-swiped-jobs-world.html

CHAPTER 13: Blondes

1. "Blonde stereotype",
Wikipedia (25 April, 2024),
https://en.wikipedia.org/wiki/Blonde_stereotype#Dumb_blonde

2. Cloversmith72, "The 'Dumb' Blonde",
Looking in the Popular Culture Mirror (March 13, 2018),
https://lookinginthepopularculturemirror.wordpress.com/2018/03/13/the-dumb-blonde/

3. "Legally Blonde",
Wikipedia (25 April, 2024),
https://en.wikipedia.org/wiki/Legally_Blonde

4. "Marilyn Monroe",
Wikipedia, (25 April, 2024),
https://en.wikipedia.org/wiki/Marilyn_Monroe

5. "Blonde Hair Percentage by Country/Blond Hair by Country 2024",
   World Population Review,
   https://worldpopulationreview.com/country-rankings/blonde-hair-percentage-by-country

6. "Blonde",
   Wikipedia (1 August, 2024),
   https://en.wikipedia.org/wiki/Blond#Historical_cultural_perceptions

7. "Brits prefer blondes: Blonde is the nation's number one dyed hair colour of choice",
   Mintel (May 2, 2018),
   https://www.mintel.com/press-centre/brits-prefer-blondes-blonde-is-the-nations-number-one-dyed-hair-colour-of-choice/

8. "Hair Color Market Size, Share & Trends Analysis Report By Product (Permanent, Temporary), By End-user, By Distribution Channel, By Region, And Segment Forecasts, 2022-2028",
   Grand View Research,
   https://www.grandviewresearch.com/industry-analysis/hair-color-market-report

9. Dea Birkett, "To dye for",
   The Guardian (25 Sep, 2001),
   https://www.theguardian.com/world/2001/sep/25/gender.uk

10. Arabelle Sicardi, "Why Going Blonde Has Never Been Just About Hair Color,"
    Allure (November 19, 2022),

https://www.allure.com/story/history-of-blonde-hair

11. Brian Bates, "The new blonde bombshell",
The Observer (29 July, 2001),
https://www.theguardian.com/theobserver/
2001/jul/29/featuresreview.review

12. Daily Mail reporter, "Blondes dyeing their hair to be taken more seriously amid recession job fears",
Daily Mail (19 March, 2009),
https://www.dailymail.co.uk/femail/article-1162665/
Blondes-dyeing-hair-taken-seriously-amid-recession-job-fears.html

13. Sarah Buckley and Amelia Butterly, "100 Women: I dye my hair brown to be taken more seriously at work",
BBC (11 September, 2017),
https://www.bbc.com/news/magazine-41082939

14. Emily Peck, "Why An Outsized Number of Blondes Are Leading The Country",
HuffPost (August 24, 2016),
https://www.huffpost.com/entry/blonde-leaders-sexism_n_57bdd4f5e4b00c67eca12176

15. Jay L. Zagorsky, Boston University, "Are Blondes Really Dumb?",
Economics Bulletin 36(1): 401-410 (March 2016),
https://www.researchgate.net/publication/
305222263_Are_Blondes_Really_Dumb

16. As/Is, "12 Everyday Problems of Blonde Girls",
YouTube (February 12, 2014),
https://www.youtube.com/watch?v=UoOG4B1_p_g

17. Dolly Parton Quotes. (n.d.).
    BrainyQuote.com. Retrieved March 28, 2024, from
    BrainyQuote.com Web site:
    https://brainyquote.com/quotes/dolly_parton_106181

CHAPTER 14: Nationality

1. The Secret Traveller, "National Stereotypes That Turn
   Out To Be True",
   1Cover Travel Insurance,
   https://www.1cover.com.au/secret-traveller/
   national-stereotypes

2. Livio Di Matteo, "Russia and its former satellites lag
   behind rest of Europe on per-capita GDP",
   Fraser Institute (March 14, 2022),
   https://www.fraserinstitute.org/blogs/russia-and-its-
   former-satellites-lag-behind-rest-of-europe-on-
   per-capita-gdp

3. V.F. Nitsevich *et al*, "Why Russia Cannot Become the
   Country of Prosperity", 2019,
   IOP Conf. Ser.: Earth Environ. Sci. **272** 032148,
   chrome-extension://efaidnbmnnnibpcajpcglclefind-
   mkaj/
   https://iopscience.iop.org/article/10.1088/1755-1315/
   272/3/032148/pdf

4. Daily Mail Reporter, "Russians snatch 'worst tourists'
   crown from Germans... even hiding sunloungers in
   their ROOMS",
   Mail Online (28 August, 2009),
   https://www.dailymail.co.uk/news/article-1209411/

Russians-snatch-worst-tourists-crown-Germans-
-hiding-sunloungers-ROOMS.html

5. Shelly Tan, "Russians are Hollywood's go-to film villains – that's unlikely to change",
   Washington Post (April 22, 2022),
   https://www.washingtonpost.com/arts-entertainment/
   2022/04/22/russians-are-hollywoods-go-to-film-vil-
   lains-thats-unlikely-change/

6. "Great Chinese Famine",
   Wikipedia (26 April, 2024),
   https://en.wikipedia.org/wiki/Great_Chinese_Famine

7. Yang Yao, "Chapter 7 - The Chinese Growth Miracle",
   Editor(s): Philippe Aghion, Steven N. Durlauf,
   Handbook of Economic Growth,
   Elsevier, Volume 2, 2014, Pages 943-1031, ISSN
   1574-0684, ISBN 9780444535467,
   https://doi.org/10.1016/B978-0-444-53540-5.00007-0,
   (https://www.sciencedirect.com/science/article/pii/
   B9780444535405000070)

CHAPTER 15: Ethnicity – a personal journey

1. "Cape Coloureds",
   Wikipedia (26 April, 2024),
   https://en.wikipedia.org/wiki/Cape_Coloureds

2. Robert Gentle,
   The Scholarship Kids
   (Cape Town: Melinda Ferguson Books, 2023)

3. "African Americans",
   Wikipedia (26 April, 2024),
   https://en.wikipedia.org/wiki/African_Americans
   #Economic_status

4. Allen J. Beck, "Race and Ethnicity of Violence Crime
   Offenders and Arrestees, 2018",
   U.S. Department of Justice, Statistical Brief (January
   2021, NCJ 255969),
   chrome-extension://
   efaidnbmnnnibpcajpcglclefindmkaj/https://
   bjs.ojp.gov/content/pub/pdf/revcoa18.pdf

5. Zhen Zeng, "Jail Inmates in 2021 – Statistical Tables",
   Bureau of Justice Statistics (December 2022),
   https://bjs.ojp.gov/library/publications/
   jail-inmates-2021-statistical-tables

6. "External factors, including homicide, drive death rate
   disparity in US black-white young adults",
   University of Oxford (11 November 2022),
   https://www.ox.ac.uk/news/2022-11-11-external-
   factors-including-homicide-drive-death-rate-
   disparity-us-black-white-young

7. "Shooting bias", *Wikipedia* (6 June, 2024),
   https://en.wikipedia.org/wiki/Shooting_bias

8. Nicole Phillip, "9 People Reveal a Time They Racially
   Stereotyped a Stranger",
   The New York Times (May 25, 2018),
   https://www.nytimes.com/2018/05/25/
   reader-center/racial-stereotypes.html

9. Kim Hjelmgaard, " 'I'm leaving, and I'm just not coming back': Fed up with racism, Black Americans head overseas",
USA Today (June 26, 2020),
https://www.usatoday.com/story/news/world/2020/06/26/blaxit-black-americans-leave-us-escape-racism-build-lives-abroad/3234129001/

CHAPTER 17: Movies
1. "Jungian archetypes",
Wikipedia (26 April, 2024),
https://en.wikipedia.org/wiki/Jungian_archetypes

2. "Collective unconscious",
Wikipedia (26 April, 2024),
https://en.wikipedia.org/wiki/Collective_unconscious

3. "Writing 101: The 12 Literary Archetypes",
MasterClass (August 30, 2021),
https://www.masterclass.com/articles/writing-101-the-12-literary-archetypes

4. WatchMojo, "Top 10 Typical Movie Character Stereotypes",
YouTube (April 2, 2015),
https://www.youtube.com/watch?v=-PR4TYzfM7Y

5. Benjamin Lindsay,
"How To Find Your Type as an Actor",
Backstage (April 12, 2021),
https://www.backstage.com/magazine/article/find-type-actor-3730/

6. "Typecasting",
Wikipedia (26 April, 2024),
https://en.wikipedia.org/wiki/Typecasting

7. "Casting (performing arts)",
Wikipedia (26 April, 2024),
https://en.wikipedia.org/wiki/
Casting_(performing_arts)

8. FoundationINTERVIEWS, "Producer Kevin Bright on
the casting process on
'Friends' – EMMYTVLEGENDS.ORG",
YouTube (April 28, 2017),
https://www.youtube.com/watch?v=MG26JAzp-MM

9. Quoteresearch, "All I Want Is a Story. If You Have a
Message, Send It by Western Union",
Quote Investigator (May 11, 2019),
https://quoteinvestigator.com/2019/05/11/send/

10. Laurie Wastell, "The year Hollywood truly lost the
plot",
Spiked (31 December, 2022),
https://www.spiked-online.com/2022/12/31/
the-year-hollywood-truly-lost-the-plot/

11. Aja Romano, "The racist backlash to The Little Mermaid and Lord of The Rings is exhausting and extremely predictable",
Vox (September 17, 2022),
https://www.vox.com/culture/23357114/
the-little-mermaid-racist-backlash-lotr-rings-of-
power-diversity-controversy

12. Alex Sherman, "Disney CEO Bob Iger says company's movies have been too focused on messaging", *CNBC* (November 30, 2023), https://www.cnbc.com/2023/11/30/disney-ceo-bob-iger-says-movies-have-been-too-focused-on-messaging.html

CHAPTER 18: Advertising
1. Stephen Leacock Quotes. (n.d.). *BrainyQuote.com*. Retrieved April 3, 2024, from BrainyQuote.com Web site: https://brainyquote.com/quotes/stephen_leacock_213382

2. Alex Mayyasi, "How an Ad Campaign Made Lesbians Fall in Love with Subaru", *Priceonomics* (May 23, 2016), https://priceonomics.com/how-an-ad-campaign-made-lesbians-fall-in-love-with/

3. Zach Lazzari, "Types of Stereotyping in Advertising", *Chron* (October 19, 2018), https://smallbusiness.chron.com/types-stereotyping-advertising-11937.html

4. Lisa Salmon, "Women do more multitasking at home while men do solo chores, study says", *The Independent* (19 April, 2023), https://www.independent.co.uk/life-style/diy-sociology-aston-university-men-rick-stein-b2322695.html

5. "2023 Bud Light boycott",

Wikipedia (26 April, 2024),
https://en.wikipedia.org/wiki/2023_Bud_Light_boycott

6. "The Best Men Can Be",
Wikipedia (26 April, 2024),
https://en.wikipedia.org/wiki/The_Best_Men_Can_Be

7. "Glass: The Lion for Change",
Cannes Lions,
https://www.canneslions.com/awards/lions/glass-the-lion-for-change

8. "Dove Campaign for Real Beauty",
Wikipedia (26 April, 2024),
https://en.wikipedia.org/wiki/Dove_Campaign_for_Real_Beauty

CHAPTER 19: Cars
1. The Wall Street Journal, "BMW Drivers Really Are Jerks, Studies Find",
YouTube (August 14, 2013),
https://www.youtube.com/watch?v=cFQsOnunSGk

2. Joy Pearson, "What does your car say about your personality?",
Quick Car Finance (20 May, 2023),
https://www.quickcarfinance.co.uk/blog/buying-a-car/what-does-your-car-say-about-your-personality/

3. Darren Cassey, "What Does Your Ride Say About You?

Here Are 13 Stereotypes",
Car Throttle (18 May 2015),
https://www.carthrottle.com/news/what-does-your-ride-say-about-you-here-are-13-stereotypes

4. Robert Hardman, "It's billed as the car all girls adore: So would our man drive them crazy with the new Fiat 500?",
Daily Mail (1 October, 2008),
https://www.dailymail.co.uk/news/article-1066303/Its-billed-car-girls-adore-So-man-drive-crazy-new-Fiat-500.html

5. Cheryl Tay, "What men and women want in a car",
yahoo! news (4 November 2011),
https://sg.news.yahoo.com/blogs/fit-to-post-autos/men-women-want-car-101600022.html

6. "Life is a highway: Study confirms cars have personality",
Florida State University News (November 26, 2008),
https://news.fsu.edu/news/business-law-policy/2008/11/26/life-highway-study-confirms-cars-personality/

7. Christian Jarrett, "Driver stereotypes",
The British Psychological Society: The Psychologist (21 February, 2005),
https://www.bps.org.uk/research-digest/driver-stereotypes

CHAPTER 20: Artificial Intelligence
1. Robot Future, "The Top 5 Female Humanoid Robots

of 2022",
YouTube (November 27, 2022),
https://www.youtube.com/watch?v=8MbaB4MuBio

2. Sylvie Borau, "Female robots are seen as being the most human. Why?",
The Conversation (April 14, 2021),
https://theconversation.com/female-robots-are-seen-as-being-the-most-human-why-158666

3. Tanya Lewis, "Rise of the Fembots: Why Artificial Intelligence Is Often Female",
Live Science (February 20, 2015),
https://www.livescience.com/49882-why-robots-female.html

4. Joanna Stern, "Alexa, Siri, Cortana: The Problem With All-Female Digital Assistants",
The Wall Street Journal (February 21, 2017),
https://www.wsj.com/articles/alexa-siri-cortana-the-problem-with-all-female-digital-assistants-1487709068

5. Ibid.

6. "Did BMW recall their GPS system due to its female voice?",
Skeptics Stack Exchange,
https://skeptics.stackexchange.com/questions/27244/did-bmw-recall-their-gps-system-due-to-its-female-voice

7. Stephen Buranyi, "Rise of the racist robots – how AI is learning all our worst impulses",

The Guardian (8 August, 2017),
https://www.theguardian.com/inequality/2017/
aug/08/rise-of-the-racist-robots-how-ai-is-
learning-all-our-worst-impulses

8. "NZ study: humans can be 'racist' towards robots, too",
NZ Herald (11 March, 2018),
https://www.nzherald.co.nz/nz/nz-study-humans
-can-be-racist-toward-robots-too/
S6TMUIHGMSN3HMJM3PNAPEIVUA/

9. "Algorithmic bias",
Wikipedia (26 April, 2024),
https://en.wikipedia.org/wiki/Algorithmic_bias

10. "Medical School Admissions: Report of a formal in-
vestigation into St. George's Hospital Medical School
(1988)",
Wikipedia (26 April, 2024),
https://en.wikipedia.org/wiki/Medical_School_
Admissions:_Report_of_a_formal_investigation_
into_St._George%27s_Hospital_Medical_School_(19
88)

11. Jeffrey Dastin, "Amazon scraps secret AI recruiting tool
that showed bias against women",
The Irish Times (October 10, 2018),
https://www.irishtimes.com/business/technology/
amazon-scraps-secret-ai-recruiting-tool-that-
showed-bias-against-women-1.3658651

12. Albert Einstein quote,
AZ Quotes,
https://www.azquotes.com/quote/465987

13. Kim Martineau, "What is generative AI?",
    IBM (20 April 2023),
    https://research.ibm.com/blog/what-is-generative-AI

14. Mathilde Desgranges, "Paris: Raphaël Enthoven remporte son duel contre ChatGPT",
    20 Minutes (15/06/2023),
    https://www.20minutes.fr/paris/4041337-20230614-paris-raphael-enthoven-remporte-duel-contre-chatgpt

15. "Share of players in the NBA from 2010 to 2023, by ethnicity",
    Statista,
    https://www.statista.com/statistics/1167867/nba-players-ethnicity/

16. Andrew Griffin, "Google takes AI image generator offline over racially diverse historical images",
    The Independent (22 February, 2024),
    https://www.independent.co.uk/tech/google-gemini-ai-images-racially-diverse-b2500730.html

17. Chris Morris, "Google halts Gemini AI image tool weeks after launch as complaints surge over 'woke', historically inaccurate depictions of people of colour",
    Fortune (February 22, 2024),
    https://fortune.com/2024/02/22/google-temporarily-pulls-down-gemini-image-generation-woke/

18. Matt Walsh, "Just When You Think The Google Gemini AI Story Can't Get Any Worse, It Does",
    Daily Wire (February 23, 2024),
    https://www.dailywire.com/news/just-when-you-

think-the-google-gemini-ai-story-cant-get-any-worse-it-does

19. Emilio Ferrara, "Eliminating bias in AI may be impossible – a computer scientist explains how to tame it instead",
The Conversation (July 19, 2023),
https://theconversation.com/eliminating-bias-in-ai-may-be-impossible-a-computer-scientist-explains-how-to-tame-it-instead-208611

20. Melissa Heikkilä, "AI language models are rife with different political biases",
MIT Technology Review (August 7, 2023),
https://www.technologyreview.com/2023/08/07/1077324/ai-language-models-are-rife-with-political-biases/

21. "Grok (chatbot)",
Wikipedia (26 April, 2024),
https://en.wikipedia.org/wiki/Grok_(chatbot)

CHAPTER 21: Humour
1. Jon Henley, " 'Crude, but rarely nasty': The jokes Europeans tell about their neighbours",
The Guardian (8 May, 2016),
https://www.theguardian.com/world/2016/may/08/crude-but-rarely-nasty-the-jokes-europeans-tell-about-their-neighbours

2. Yanko Tsvetkov,
Atlas of Prejudice: The Complete Stereotype Map Collection (Alphadesigner, 2016),

https://www.amazon.com/Atlas-Prejudice-Complete-Stereotype-Collection/dp/8461795660/

3. *"Mad* (magazine)",
Wikipedia (26 April, 2024),
https://en.wikipedia.org/wiki/Mad_(magazine)

4. Gershon Legman,
Rationale of the Dirty Joke: An Analysis of Sexual Humor (New York: Grove Press, 1968),
https://www.amazon.com/Rationale-Dirty-Joke-Analysis-Sexual/dp/0743292529/

5. Max Eastman Quotes. (n.d.).
BrainyQuote.com. Retrieved March April 5, 2024, from
BrainyQuote.com Web site: https://brainyquote.com/quotes/max_eastman_163703

www.ingramcontent.com/pod-product-compliance
Lightning Source LLC
Chambersburg PA
CBHW072133020426
42334CB00018B/1789